Indians
at Work
and Play

Other books by the author:

Travel Trails at Home and Abroad
Red Man's Trail
Indian Cultures of the Southwest
The Quakers of Iowa
Aboriginal American Oratory
Highlights of Puebloland
So Say the Indians

Indians at Work and Play

by Louis Thomas Jones, Ph.D.

The Naylor Company
Book Publishers of the Southwest
San Antonio, Texas

In Memory
of
JAMES FRANCIS THORPE

Better known in the Sauk-Fox Indian
tongue as *Ma-Tho-Huck*, or Bright Path.

For America's "Golden Age of Sports" Jim Thorpe's
name was a household word. From Carlisle Indian School,
Pennsylvania, Bright Path represented our First Americans
in the world Olympics, Stockholm, Sweden, 1912. In both
its pentathlon and decathlon categories, he scored many
firsts.

A descendant of the famed Iowa Chief Black Hawk,
Bright Path loved sports life. Strong of body and mind,
he proved himself a winner. Today, in bronze, seven feet
high, his statue rests in the rotunda of America's Pro Football Hall of Fame, Canton, Ohio, poised in action. Hence
Ma-Tho-Huck will be remembered as long as America's
love for sports life lasts.

Jim Thorpe Statue

Preface

OFTEN WHILE WORKING on the materials which were built into two of my earlier publications, *Aboriginal American Oratory* and *So Say the Indians*, companions each to the other, I had wondered how our first Americans of pre-Columbian days spent their leisure time, if they had such. From childhood to the present, mine has been a busy life. Along the way it has been filled with many thrilling experiences both at home and abroad as I have rambled over our earth.

Until I came to know better, my mental image of America's red men was this: they were of a sombre nature, glum, sullen, fond of displaying their eagle feathers and adorned costumes in public, but inactive, except in war. What a body brand! What a mental image!

But travel and firsthand knowledge of our red men's ways have changed these adverse impressions with me. As for my interest in his aboriginal playlife, unblemished by influences from his outer world, it came about in this way. Shuffling through dry government records stored on library shelves, I came upon a volume titled *Bureau of American Ethnology Report, 24*. It purported to be a study of American Indian playlife of the pre-Columbian era, about which I knew next to nothing. Even the text itself had been published almost three-quarters of a century before.

Historically minded, naturally I reacted to its content much like a needle does to its pulling magnet. Immediately our interests were bound together and became one. And with it, my image of our first Americans, playwise, changed for the better. It brought me into immediate contact with the traditional recreational culture of our native Indian peoples, continent wide. The vast quantity of research data presented in the above mentioned *Report, 24,* covering all parts of North America, was classified under three main heads. These were amusement games largely played around home fires; games intended to develop muscular skills of action and dexterity; and finally, games which involved risk taking and elements of chance. These three bore the brunt of no less than five years of the close expert study of many persons; and these three categories form the substance of the pages here to be presented.

To aid the reader as our story advances, citations to sources used and details mentioned find expression by a number system used in our "Notes and References," arranged at the close of our work. Each citation carries its own number, found first on its printed page. This method also provided a convenient way of acknowledging "permission to use," granted by the owners of copyrights.

In connection with this monograph, my thanks first is due to the head librarian of Whittier College. It was he who twice secured the loan of *Report, 24* from the California State Library, Sacramento, California, for my use. With its content I labored day and night, fully aware of its great value as a discovery almost unknown to the general public. In addition many similar works of comparable reliability were examined and used in connection with the product

viii

at hand. Likewise, invaluable data was supplied by such institutions as Haskell Institute, Lawrence, Kansas, our federal government's Department of Health, Education, and Welfare, as well as our far-flung U.S. Bureau of Indian Affairs, and kindred agencies.

The staff members of Southwest Museum, Los Angeles, California, specialists in this field, guided my trail as this project developed. So, too, with many individuals, some of whom were Indians, some non-Indians. Outstanding among these was Wallace J. Newman of Luiseño extraction, known for his athletic achievements and ability. Another was Robert L. Bennett, former Commissioner of American Indian Affairs, now professor of law at the University of New Mexico at Albuquerque. A third was Chief C. Lorenzo Big Canoe, head of the Chippewas of Georgina Island, Ontario, Canada, along with other red men of like standing. Capable white counsellors likewise were numerous — all of whom hereby have my enduring thanks.

Now this product goes forth to meet its fate. If it is worthy, it will succeed. If it is stilted and uninteresting, however valuable, it too may find lodgement on dusty library shelves. At least its builder has been enlightened. Never again will he hold a stereotyped image of our aboriginal Americans. They were real people, worthy ancestors of their progeny and successors.

Today their offspring are pioneers of tomorrow. Heading their ranks as leaders, many hold positions of high trust in governmental posts of responsibility. Some are skilled business executives; others grace our law courts as attorneys and justices; many are artists of renown. Within the past decade at least ten have come up as Nobel Prize winners in various fields of literature and science, some specialists even in nuclear science. Many have found placement in the healing arts: applied medicine, trained nursing and dentistry. Others have prospered as skilled cattle raisers, agricultural experts, and machinists of all kinds, while others support the armed forces of our great nation.

A few years ago this body of our citizenry in point of numbers was looked upon as a vanishing race. However, not so now! While they are one of the smallest of our minorities amidst our growing composite population, their increase has been surprising. Today the United States has within its borders approximately 500,000 persons who carry enough American Indian blood in their veins to classify as red men. And in the Dominion of Canada to the north there are half as many more, not to mention the aboriginals of countries to the south of our Mexican national line.

These are America's red men of the future. For ages uncounted they and their forbears have proved their endurance and fearlessness in times of peril and racial need. And to them our New World must continue to cling for that strength and genius which they alone numerically can supply.

This is the summary of our findings. This is the conviction to which we are driven. This is the why of our story. As it blazes its way over land and sea, we trust that its purpose will be understood. Its author has no apology to offer for his fellow red Americans. They are worthy of the confidence of our nation's best. Evidence of the past clearly shows that when emergency arises they can be trusted to keep America, their paternal land, safe and strong for their progeny wherever found, irrespective of tribal loyalties and the social strains of the hour. This is nature's way. This is the way of humanity. Let the curtain now lift for scenes that lie before us and events yet to be!

Louis Thomas Jones

Acknowledgments

TO BRING THE DEEP CHASM which separates pre-Columbian times from today's interests, play and work-wise, has been the author's problem. Of course, like other workmen, he has to depend upon specialists in many fields for much of his factual material used. Here these are, in the main, acknowledged.

For example: The first page of our theme mentions "83 billion dollars" as America's estimated fun bill for the year 1969. It appeared in Vol. 67, No. 11, pages 58-59 of the *U.S. News & World Report*. Mr. Audrey L. Forbes stood as manager of its news service. Gladly he issued its permit of usage. So, too, with many other publishers, institutions, and individuals, each of whom gave as ready assent.

Among these nation and continent wide, the following are here gratefully named. The Royal Bank of Canada, Montreal, said this of the Dominion's aboriginal Americans: "These are real people." Permission was readily given to quote. So with many others. Numerous institutions, local and national, extended a helping hand. So the work went on.

Mr. Wallace E. Galluzzi, Superintendent of Haskell

(Indian) Institute, Lawrence, Kansas, scanned our document and evaluated its content for its cover. So, also, did Dr. William A. Burns, Director of the National Museum of Man, San Diego, California, so all could read.

From Canton, Ohio, home of America's Pro Football Hall of Fame, also came the picture of its favored First American, James Francis Thorpe, winner of Olympic honors at Stockholm, Sweden, 1912. A Sauk-Fox Indian, by similar grant, his image attends our dedicatorial page.

Southwest Museum, Los Angeles, with its able staff headed by its Drector, Dr. Carl S. Dentzel, assisted as our document took shape. Again and again, in scope and scholarship, this assistance proved invaluable.

Moreover, numerous local and state libraries yielded assistance to this venture. The Bonnie Bell Wardman Library of Whittier College, Whittier, California, is one of these. So, too, with the efficient staff and the loaded shelves of the Los Angeles Public Library. But when more singular documents were needed, these came gratis from the California State Library, Sacramento. Without such facilities this venture of ours would have been futile. In this way its chinks were filled in when needed. To each of the above agencies, public and private, comes the thanks of its author.

As for individuals who assisted, their number is legion. Heading this group was Louis R. Bruce, United States Commissioner of Indian Affairs. Firsthand, for my information, he submitted the needed data relative to his cultural background and valued career. This was shared with me in my attempt to understand Amerindian problems studied in this document.

Likewise the life sketch of W. W. Keeler, head Chief of the Oklahoma Cherokee Nation, proved of singular value for the purposes of our text *Indians at Work and*

xii

Play. As a native, having risen from the ranks, he speaks the mind of coordinate modern America. His counsel to today's composite youth carries impelling truth as expressed in our closing pages.

As to others upon whose shoulders the author has leaned heavily, brevity is demanded. First stands my friend Wallace J. Newman, a native son of California. Born on the La Jolla Reservation, but a short distance from San Diego of our Southland, his counsel and guidance was priceless. A graduate of the University of Southern California, Los Angeles, for years he served as head football coach at Whittier College. Also his outreach, statewide, has been tremendous in Amerindian affairs.

Another native Indian aide of wide experience has been George Pierre, scholar and writer. Chief of the Colville Federated Indian Tribes of the Walla Walla Country, State of Washington. He is the moving spirit and promoter of the All American Indian Week movement, dedicated to the educational interests of his people. He, too, is a university graduate, a leader of high repute and organizational ability. Of course among my many Indian aides there are women of standing. One of these is Mrs. Lela Kiana Oman, a proud Eskimo, whose home is in Nome, Alaska. Her grants to quote, indeed, were generous.

As has often been said, few readers are aware as to how books actually come to be. But the writers know in part. First comes the choice of a theme, then the gathering of its material. When ready, a publisher must be found. Next comes the strain of editing, then its art work, and finally, the book itself. This is how books are born. This is how their content is made immortal. This is why thanks to those who help is due. Hence our "Acknowledgment"! It is our thanks to all who had a part in its making.

Louis Thomas Jones

Contents

xvi

The Scene Opens

RECENTLY THIS HEADER appeared in a nationwide publication of standing, together with its thrilling story. Its first words read this way:

83 Billion Dollars For Leisure[1]

What a statement! Who ever saw *one billion dollars* in one place at one time? Perhaps this could be done in yellow gold, at Fort Knox, Kentucky, the treasure chest of the United States government. But what about eighty-three billion dollars — all spent in one year for leisure or for fun? Let us break this vast sum down into its component

1

parts and see where these dollars went. In a way, this may reflect how Americans today engineer their leisure-time pursuits, and what they deem most important. Over against our findings we may then place judgement on how our first Americans of bygone days utilized their leisure time in playways well known to them.

One of these items, and its leading one, was thirty-five billion dollars. It was for vacations and joy trips at home. Next came five billion for travel abroad. This is understandable in view of the educational value of such travel and the seeing of strange things in foreign lands. Strangely enough, eleven billion went for private airplanes, bicycles, auto-campers, snowmobiles and the like. Added to these, nine billion were charged to the purchase of radio sets, T.V., records, and musical instruments of many kinds. This, in part, was America's one year fun spree, spent almost without a quiver of conscience as to where it went.

What lies ahead? If ten years hence America's pace of population increases in keeping with its 1960-1970 decade, what will it be by 1980? About this problem every fabric of our nation is concerned. Our toy shops are concerned about it. Our steamship companies, our clothing suppliers, our food markets, our farming population, our photographers, our bus builders, our telephone operators, our bookmakers, yes, our workers of every description are concerned. But look to the year 2000. What will our youth and our adult population be then? Only the gods of the future can tell.

As for the grass roots from which America's leisure-time urges have sprung, this calls for a backward glance. Such a search takes us to our earliest colonial days; then to the rise of the white's cultures of Europe, and beyond. Then follows our study of our aboriginal American cul-

2

tures, those of our so-called American Indian peoples, so varied in origin and development.

This is a heavy assignment for short space, we know, but this is what lies ahead. This is our purpose. This is our quest.

America's Curtain Rises

I T IS TRITE TO SAY that on Friday, October 12, 1492, Christopher Columbus first set foot on American soil. Almost every American child knows this today. To Columbus that was his discovery day. But did he know where he was? Did he have any concept of the size and the natural wealth of the region found? It will be recalled that when he took back to Spain a few of the natives met, evidently he called them Indians, thinking that he had been to ancient east *India*, not new America. In this way America's red men acquired their name *American* Indians, it seems.

And let us be reminded that, in general, European

countries, like Spain, were in their colonial day. England, France, Belgium, Holland, and Italy, were agog (drunk) with the spirit of colonialism. In fact, European peoples had risen to their position of wealth and power as they plied their trade between what then was their west and the far away east.

Each of these nations had its own institutions, its own language, its own pastimes and pleasures, its own ways of doing things. Each had its own castles and cathedrals, its own ships exploiting the ocean waves, and its own homes and gardens, together with its own festivities to be enjoyed and fostered. In other words, Europe then was little interested in what was primeval America.

After Columbus' discovery day, it took Europe almost two hundred years, strangely enough, to awaken to the resources of the Americas and the life's interests of their red sons and daughters. To Europeans, they knew nothing of the culture and the leisure-time activities enjoyed by them for unknown centuries of time, as measured by Europeans far, far away.

Then the discovery curtain of European consciousness of where the world's wealth lay, dawned upon the European mind. Europe's future destiny lay not in the far east, but in the west — the lands of the setting sun. Its gold, its fabulous furs, its lumber, its vast fisheries, its trade with its primitive peoples called loudly to European ears. Hence Europe's face turned west for its era of future colonization.

From that time on, European monarchs strove with one another for possessions in this our New World. With a vehemence previously unknown among mortals, hither they came by the tens, the hundreds, the thousands — here to endure the hardships of primitive lands and to pile up their cumulative wealth. It is necessary for us to comprehend these facts in order to understand the racial struggle which here followed. This, too, is a part of our story.

6

Red Men See
Whites Coming

HOW PRIMITIVE AMERICANS got their generic name *Indian* has been explained. Today this name covers our aborigines from Cape Horn, South America, to the tip of the Bering Strait, which presses hard against the Arctic Circle far to the north, North America. In this one factor, at least, these two vast continents are joined in European minds. How the *culture image* of America's red men has become a fixture to the white man's world, however, needs explanation. This let us attempt.

History tells us that the Spanish were the first to colonize in America. Their initial settlement was made at St. Augustine, Florida. The very name *Florida* carries its attraction. This came from the hand of the romantic Ponce de Leon, its explorer, in the year 1512. Its name meant "The Feast of Flowers," for that was Spain's Easter Sunday.

The English established themselves at Jamestown, Virginia, almost a century later. Its land was the home of the famed Pocahontas who won Capt. John Smith's affections here in America's wilds. That was the year 1607, if our colonial calender rings true. However, shortly thereafter, a victim of smallpox, in Smith's homeland, England, this princely young woman paid the price for her wooing and was laid to rest in English soil far, far from her childhood home.

Dutch and French sea rovers took to the lands to the north of Jamestown and those of the Massachusetts Bay Company. Their searchings led them to the St. Lawrence River Basin, Quebec and Montreal, one of the wildest of scenes known to North America. Their motives of urgency, in the main, appear to have been two. One was hides of fur-bearing animals of forests and streams: their destination — the backs of French nobility, lords and ladies. The other — the souls of primitive untaught Americans, urged on by those in Europe, headed by His Holiness, The Pope, at Rome. These two passions motivated much of French exploitation of our red men's America.

Eastern red men watched this invasion of white Europeans with anxious eyes, we may be sure. As portrayed in stone by a sculptor from our far west, when the whites first came to New England's shores, red men greeted them with open arms and fed them. Soon disillusioned, however, those open hands turned to closed fists. Next those same hands carried implements of war and death. Finally, overwhelmed by numbers, astride his steed, his spokesman's outstretched

8

hands were open to the skies in his appeal for protection by The Great Spirit, The Great Mystery, the maker and controller of men everywhere.[2]

This, in brief, has been the red man's experience with the European from time's start. Now as a minority group in the land of his birth, he stands astounded at the number of those who have come from all parts of our earth. Still he has lessons to teach this horde of humanity, if they will listen. Especially is this true of his legends, his customs, the deities worshipped, his basic culture—(simple but praiseworthy) — his prime folk stories suited to all of life, even his sports and playlife — the object of our immediate study and concern.

A Fixed Indian Image

THE FIXED IMAGE, carried by both the white man as well as by the red man toward each other, has stood adverse to the best interest of both since these two racial groups first met.

From the start, America's red men have been considered as inferiors by the whites. They were a people to be evangelized, displaced, brought under control. With the early white settlers, as often stated, "the only good Indian was the dead Indian." His image was that of a killer, a wild man, a being incapable of refined yearnings and desires. In his right hand, figuratively speaking, he carried his deadly tomahawk and in his left, his bloody scalping

11

knife. These instruments were dreaded by white frontier families as they moved into the wild west.

My childhood day carried this same mental image. In my hometown we had one small barbershop. At its front door, day and night, stood motionless its wooden Indian. In its hand was that same tomahawk. Its scalping knife, too, much to my horror, was there. Even our modern movie world has not helped this image much for the childhood of the present hour.

And even more, one of my intimate Indian friends, an ex-serviceman of our World War II, has told me of this his own experience. On reaching homeland shores from Europe, within the shadow of old Faneuil Hall close to where my own mother grew to womanhood, Boston, Massachusetts, seeing his red skin, children yelled this their taunt. Said they: "You low-lived Kickapoo. Kill the dirty Indian!"[3] This was his reward for his skin color.

On the other hand, to the Indian mind the white man's image suffered like distortion. Basically, he was a land grabber. With his gun, ever at his side, he too was a killer. His worship centered in a book, called by him the Bible, not in nature. Not until I sat beside the shaman, the village priest of old Zuñi, New Mexico, at the top of Thunder Mountain, Zuñi's sacred shrine, our feet dangling over its precipice-like walls, did I see through this image. This was the occasion.

We were up there to look for ancient Zuñi artifacts. The sun was setting. The west was aglow with coloration, like that of mingled rainbows. Both of us were silenced by the glory, indescribable, before us. In my ignorance I broke silence. I mumbled this: "How I wish I possessed the skill of the artist! I would put on canvas this matchless scene." This was his response: "Just like white man. Always wants to reduce nature to paper. Indian senses beauty within and

12

is satisfied." Again, silence. That was all. Then and there, I learned my lesson.

Whatever the situation may be, through all ages of the past red men as well as white men have been *homo sapiens*, or human beings. That much, at least, we know.

Red men hate. Red men love. They laugh; they cry. They sing together, and when trouble comes they worry, like all of humanity. And they also worked and played, as soon we shall see. Of them the Royal Bank of Canada said this to its many patrons of America's red men. This is what that institution said:

> These are real people, not fruits of the imagination of strip artists, movie writers and book authors. They are not men and women in chorus-girl costumes whose destiny it is to entertain us, but people seeking what people everywhere seek — home, health, and happiness.

> The majority of these native people stand neither in one world nor the other. They are enmeshed in the old culture while trying to take advantage of the new way of life introduced from abroad. They are freedom loving people, resenting dependency. Their economic problems are as serious as those facing the newly emerging nations of Africa[4] . . .

and elsewhere. This is today's status of almost a million red men who live astride the imaginary line which separates the Dominion of Canada and The United States of America. But playwise, our concerns are those of the ancient day, a time before any known white man had set foot on America's soil.

Words to be Objectified

TO GET A CORRECT view of that which lies ahead, it is important that together we carry clear meanings of certain current terms to be used. Should it be any occupation such as farming, working with livestock or cattle, perhaps bookkeeping or in the business world, engineering, trained nursing, the law, medicine, or otherwise — the same will be true. Each specialty today has its own vocabulary. Even in athletics on today's playing field the terms used must for us have their meaning or we cannot function aright. The following are some of these terms.

Since we are to get a glimpse into the red man's pre-Columbian past we shall need to be familiar with the science of anthropology. In its essence it deals with matters that are ages old. It is the science of the origin of man, his customs, his beliefs, and the development of his many life's practices. We can see how this must apply to the task at hand.

Another of these social sciences is that of ethnology. It parallels the field of anthropology, interested as its workers are in the institutions, the characteristics, the distribution, and the culture of human beings and the many kindred relationships which have to do with their welfare.

Linguistics is a third term with which we should be on speaking terms. It is almost self-explained. When we realize that almost every tribal group of red men, as dwellers on the American continent, had its own language, the importance of having specialists who are familiar with the meaning of the word-sounds used will make clear the part they have to play in the study at hand.

Of course there are related fields of study which should be known to our work, but these will be defined as we come to them. One of these is the term *artifact.*

An artifact, by the way, is defined as being anything made by human skill or work. Come into my study and I will show you one. It serves me as a door stop. It keeps my study door from banging, as blowing winds come and go. It is a stone. At one edge it is about two inches broad. At its opposite edge it tapers down to less than a quarter of an inch thick. What do you think it might be? As to where it came from, I do not know. As to its age, this much is certain: It was not made yesterday. It must be eons old. It is similar to those found in museums and Indian wigwams in many parts of our vast country. Yes, it is an artifact.

And I have another artifact close by. In a word, let me tell you about it. It is made of wood, not stone. In shape it resembles the Irish shillelagah, used as a defense weapon in the Emerald Isle across the seas. Clearly, it was made by red man's hands. It is about fourteen inches in length, slightly curved at its tip. Its handle is roughened a bit to prevent skipping when thrown. An experienced anthropologist has told me that it was used by red men in their gaming for small birds or rabbits for food. Knowing the skill of Indian arms in throwing, as I do, I could credit this artifact as of use in the purpose suggested.

Another instrument of common household usage was the *metate*. It, too, speaks of ancient times. In the far west it was to be found in almost every wickiup and household. It was a stone about twelve by fourteen inches in size, used as a base on which the family ground its maize or corn for its daily meal. So the forms and types of artifacts common to the red man's home of the early day were almost endless in number.

Now we should turn to certain ideas and concepts carried in the early red man's way of life, known to every scientist or specialist in this field. The first of these is the term *figurines*; another is *pictographs*; and still another is *petroglyphs*. All three of these call for a word of explanation.

Figurines are of many kinds. Usually they are symbols of mystical figures connected in some way with primitive or barbaric worship. With our first Americans, generally speaking, they might be made of wood or stone, or even of hardened clay or like materials. They may represent a wolf, a deer, a bear, or even birds or creeping creatures. These figurines usually are found in infrequented caves or other formations protected against weathering. If made of wood, usually they give evidence of having been treated with a preservative similar to our lacquer used for like purposes today. True figurines are among the oldest of

17

our artifacts found now. With the ancients they were supposed to carry divination or spirit powers.

A pictograph is a drawing painted or scratched on stone or some enduring carrier. Of course, they were made long before modern photography was known. Pictographs usually, like figurines, are found in caves, though here and there throughout North America as well as in European lands, they decorate bare stone walls or even heaps of stones used as shrines or sacred spots. Petroglyphs, in turn, are strictly rock carvings, crude in their workmanship, but clearly representing prehistoric times.

Our Government
Takes A Hand

R ECENTLY I ENTERED a collegiate library. Under my arm was a fairly large government publication. Its outside cover carried this title: *24th Annual Report of the Bureau of American Ethnology*.[5] It was published in the year 1907. Its pages, double size, numbered 846 in all, much of which is in small print. Its content was named *Games of the North American Indians*, assembled by a scholar of his time, Steward Curlin by name.

On mentioning the book's topic, the librarian gasped: "What! Do the Indians know how to play?" With our quote in mind from the monthly letter published by the Royal Bank of Canada which we have read, my response was this: "How do you think our First Americans, young and old, spent their leisure time?" Again, to my surprise, she said: "Did the Indians have leisure time?" Leaving her desk, I assured her that to my best knowledge our Indo-Americans of bygone days did not carry the image known to our first American whites. Like ourselves, from their earliest days, they were real people. Like others the world over, they, too, played, as we shall see.

World travelers tell us that wherever found, the young of certain kinds of animals play. So, too, with humans throughout the Americas, both North and South. The Asians do it. The Africans do it. The cultured Caucasians of ancient India do it — as likewise did the Greeks, the Romans, and most Europeans throughout recorded time. Indeed, with humans, to play appears to be instinctive, if we may use this term.

So it turns out that the ethnologist studied the playlife of our aboriginal Americans through the artifacts left behind, as we have seen. Indeed, while few records were kept of their gamelife until recent years, today we know much of how and why they played, as they did; and the more we know of their sports and playlife, the more it appears to have been purposive and beneficial to their day and times.

From earliest infancy the development of the aboriginal child was supervised with great care. The universal prevalence of the Indians' board cradle gives evidence of this fact. While largely abandoned now, in bygone days it was almost a must in every household and with every mother. And more, it was common practice with these primitive Americans that every child had not only a mother, but also a god-mother — shall we call her, to watch over its

20

growth and development. That cradle gave to the adult his bearing.

Again, as for playlife and social culture, this also was virtually predetermined. As safeguards, children were taught how to place their feet in walking: no spreading of feet sidewise. Stones and bramble bushes in their trailways were too many for that. They were to walk straight and to keep their eye on their footpath. Moreover, the ball of the foot was to go down first, the heel to follow. This cushioned the upper body and lengthened life.

Where there was water, Indian children, moreover, were taught to swim. Also as a self-protective measure for later life, to play with bow and arrow, as such, were used early in both boy life and girl life. And as added safeguards, growing youth was schooled to recognize serpents that were hazardous and those which were not, showing due regard for the traditional sanctity of such in their people's mythology. And one more item. In the early intermingling of the sexes, unclothed and unabashed, boys played with girls until puberty arrived. Then for the welfare of the clan and tribal group, adult supervision came into vogue. This gives us a touch of native Indian life as it was in the long ago, a lure which could lead us far from our major interests were we to permit it so. Let us now return to how our government took a hand in raising the curtain on aboriginal sportsmanship as it was previous to the coming of European whites in so far as reliable evidence reminds in such matters. This appears to be how this matter happened.

The Stage Set
for Exploration

WITH THE OPENING of the Twentieth Century, the absorption of our aboriginal Americans into our general body politic, both north and south of the Canadian line, was well advanced. Similar governmental provisions had been established to this end, the reservation system, by both the Dominion of Canada and the United States government for the welfare of all. Each had gone its own way in treating problems of absorption and integration, with little regard to the preservation of those worthy traits of the red man's cultural heritage so

23

important to his native welfare. Especially was this true of the red man's game life, and how he spent his leisure time. Therefore, little wonder at the questions asked by our librarian mentioned.

Somewhat like the opening era of our United States government, at the beginning of the 19th century, we had a corps of master minds ready for the task at hand. In the period of building our Constitution, a century and a quarter before, it was George Washington, Thomas Jefferson, Alexander Hamilton, Benjamin Franklin, and like geniuses. At the close of the past century it was such scholars as the famed Maj. J. W. Powell, W. H. Holmes, Dr. Walter J. Fewkes, Frederick W. Hodge, who put together this capacity. For fully five years they worked at their task; *The Handbook Of American Indians,*[9] and others of like and from their hands came the volume which I had carried under my arm. It is to such authoritative studies that we must turn should we want to know how America's red men played and lived before the white's invasion came to our New World.

Where the Searchers Went

A S TO WHERE THE specialists at hand were to go, two or three guidelines early were settled upon. One of these was language familiarity, without it even a specialist could scarcely be expected to do good work. Another was that of knowing the history and culture of the tribal groups to be studied. Still a third vital necessity was to know personally some of the leaders of the peoples to be visited, for let us be reminded that red men are a proud and suspicious people, especially so when it comes to revealing their secrets to a person of different skin color, whomever he might be. These three factors formed the crux of getting the facts about the problems to be studied.

25

Sufficient to say that those best suited to know conditions along our Atlantic Rim chose that field. Others went north into the St. Lawrence Valley and the Hudson Bay country. Some went into our Great Lakes region; others to our prairie lands, the home of the bison and wandering warriors. Still others, schooled to Puebloland and its varied people went there. Among these were the noble hearted Mrs. Matilda Coxe Stevenson, an archeologist and trained nurse who spent more than a decade in that wild country, winning her way into the hearts of its strange but gifted people.

Of course our Pacific Rim had its chosen human surveyors. In what today is California alone there were no less than a hundred or more clans or tribal groups, each with its own language and dialect, together with the varied linguistic stocks from which these dialects had been derived.

And as for the far north, the dwellers on Alaskan and Arctic shores, only those of rugged vitality capable of weathering the long winters of that clime, could hope to make inroads in the study of its peoples' ways of life, even though their culture traits might be both alluring and winsome. And so who and where each of these specialists were to go in search of their Holy Grail was a serious matter. However, the old axiom, "All's well that ends well," could be applied in this case. Perhaps there has never been as thorough a study of prehistoric sportslife made, before or since, than is this one. In its essence, it was a monumental achievement. It stands alone in its value and magnitude.

In final summary, its report reads this way. All evidence evaluated, says its tabulator, "There is no evidence that any of the games described were imported into America at any time before or after the Conquest. On the other hand, they appear to be the direct and natural outgrowth of aboriginal institutions in America. They show no modification due to white influence other than the decay which characterizes all Indian institutions under existing conditions."[7]

26

Three Types Found

OF THE MANY HUNDREDS of games played by pre-Columbian Americans, continent-wide, local or regional, individually or collectively, these were all classified under three main headings or categories. These were games of chance, games of dexterity and games of amusement, as indicated in their grouping below.

Naturally, in any such arrangement there would be overlappings. That which would motivate one group in the far north in its last resort to a given contest, individual or collective, might be altogether different with the red men of the Great Lakes or the Mexican gulf areas. But with

27

the group in charge there were reasons for the placement given.

As for the Indian's chance games we need to remember that in general America's red men were animists, not deists, as were the Caucasian whites of Europe. They thought inwardly, not objectively. They, in general, were introverts, not extroverts. They were obsessed with the thought of a spirit-filled world, dominated by their supreme deity, their Great Spirit, their Great Holy, their Great Mystery. In fact they conceived of the universe about them as filled with spirit personalities of every kind, good and bad. As an illustration of this aboriginal tenet, expressed by the saintly Chief Seattle (for whom the city of Seattle, Washington, later was named), spokesman for the Dwamish tribe of Puget Sound region, as he spoke at the memorable Port Elliott Treaty of 1855. Said he:

> "There was a time when our people covered the whole land as the waves of the wind-ruffled sea covered its shell-paved floor. . . . I will not mourn over our untimely decay.
> "Your religion was written on tablets of stone, by the iron finger of your God, lest you forget it. . . . Our religion is the traditions of our ancestors, the dreams of our old men, given them by the Great Spirit. . . .
> "Every part of this country is sacred to my people. Every hillside, every valley, every plain and grove has been hallowed by some fond memory. . . . Even the rocks which seem to lie dumb as they swelter in the sun . . . thrill with memories of past events connected with the fate of my people."[8]

Thus Seattle continued as he pictured the returning hosts of his people to the hills and dales once loved and cherished, later converted to paved streets and lighted highways.

This concept of animistic control lies basic to all that the red man did and said before his brush with European Christianity, likewise acquired from eastern quarters. To him it was his way of life. He believed in the Great Spirit, the Great Mystery, the Great Holy — that which pervaded all things. To him, as earlier stated, he believed in an endless world of spirits, good and bad. All of life, to him, was a mystery. It was nature's way. It was his law of life. Hence, if he won in his gaming, the results were in full keeping with the will of the Great Spirit. If he lost, it was no sin in terms of the white man's way of thinking. It, too, was nature's way. Remember our Thunder Mountain experience at sunset! For ages past, red men have thought subjectively, not objectively. In this, their thought patterns, their culture, have been different than those of the whites. This, to them, has been their way of life.

Tabulated Index of
Games Studied

IN THE INDEX OF the games studied, these were tabulated under the three categories mentioned. Naturally there were many, many other games observed; but we have to be satisfied with the report given. This list here attends.[9]

Modified somewhat, to be sure, numerous of the games here reported continue to be played by our Indo-Americans in all parts of our North American continent in their adapted form. This is as true with the Seminoles of the Everglades of Florida as it is of the Eskimo peoples of cold, but romantic Alaska.

31

Games of chance					Games of dexterity														Minor amusements
	Guessing games								Ball										
Dice games	Stick games	Hand game	Four-stick game	Hidden ball game, or Moccasin	Archery	Snow-snake	Hoop and pole	Ring and pin	Racket	Shinney	Double ball	Ball race	Football	Hand-and-foot ball	Tossed ball	Foot-cast ball	Ball juggling	Hot ball	Shuttlecock

Minor amusements (right column):

- Shuttlecock
- Tipcat
- Quoits
- Stone-throwing
- Shuffleboard
- Jackstraws
- Swing
- Stilts
- Tops
- Bull-roarer
- Buzz
- Popgun
- Bean shooter
- Cat's cradle
- Unclassified games
- Games derived from Europeans
- Running races

It should be noted that there were but five games of chance, or guessing games assigned to the chart's first category.

The games of dexterity, however, include fourteen in all, ten of which represented some form of ball usage, large or small.

The games of minor amusement likewise here given, number fourteen in all, but, as could be assumed, these must have been almost numberless.

However, we find added to the above sports unclassified games, games smacking of European origin, as well as foot racing games, but of no horse racing because that was before the European horse, as such, was known to America's red men.

In the playing of our mixed games of today on our gridirons or football fields, our basketball floors, our skating rinks, our marksmanship contests, our many baseball diamonds, our swimming contests for young and old, our boating rivalries of many kinds, we are constantly reminded of the artistry and skills developed in these same lines before America's firstborns met the whites from the rising sun.

To be sure, Europeans had their games peculiar to their part of the earth. So, also, did the Romans, the Greeks, the eastern Asians, and the primitives of Africa, as well as the islands of the oceans. But our interests lie in those activities, and sportswise, that presumption declares they were indigenous or original with our New World, North and South. Hence let us explore our native offering and be satisfied.

Games Cited in Our Amusement List

I T IS AN AGE OLD axiom that it is as natural for an infant to play as it is for the matured leaf to fall to the ground. Who has not seen the baby first find its own fingers, then its toes, then smile with the pleasure of playing with both? You see, he has discovered his own.

So with children of every race and color. To play comes naturally with life's early years. It is as natural as it is for the sun to shine above the clouds or as for rain to fall. So it was with the red man's children as with all others.

The fourteen native American games of amusement

35

named by our group of government specialists, as seen, are these: shuttlecock, tipcat, quoits, stone-throwing, shuffleboard, jackstraws, swimming sports, stilts, the use of tops, the bull-roarer, buzz — whatever that may have been, pop-gun operation, the bean shooter, cat's cradle. All of these are classed as "minor amusements". But are these all that the pre-Columbians and their children had with which to while away their leisure time? The answer must be no. As the old saying goes, these fourteen free-time activities must have been but a drop in the bucket of the number found; but even for our investigators their limited space blocked the way for their giving us more.

The vast number of durable artifacts made of wood or stone or other materials which are stored away in our many, many museums and kindred institutions, reminders of this playlife of our early Americans, well support this assumption. The Smithsonian Institution in Washington, D.C., whose floor space seems clogged with such deposits, together with like centers such as the Queen's Museum of Toronto, Canada, and the Museum of Natural History of New York City, lead to this same conclusion. Moreover, almost every state in the United States, as well as with almost every province of Mexico, and all of the provinces of the Dominion of Canada, for decades have shared in this same collector's lure.

One such artifact came my way a few years ago. It was a preserved section of a sugar cane reed, about eight inches long. With some kind of a sharpened instrument three holes had been cut in its length below its mouth piece. Clearly it had been used as a breath instrument of the early day — an ancient flute, if you please.

Imagine the sound which it made! I put its mouth piece to my lips and blew. The note made, unobstructed, carried one pitch. Then with one finger I closed one of its openings.

Its tone quickly changed. Then I used two fingers with like results. Was I playing on a flute which had wooed some brown-eyed maiden to life's happiness in a tepee or wigwam or igloo of the long ago? Of course, I did not know. But soon it found placement on the shelves of Southwest Museum, Los Angeles, there to lure others to like speculation. By so doing, however, by imagination we try to reconstruct the many amusements and anxieties of ancient bygone days.

Stone Throwing

Glance back on our amusement activities and the composite word stone-throwing is there. In childhood's day, who has not thrown stones, either for fun or in self-defense?

Stones are found almost everywhere. And many, indeed, are the uses to which they may be put. Some are used to build homes and bridges, temples to the gods, or a thousand other things known to us all. But as for me of my boyhood game, frog-on-the-rock perhaps came down from America's pre-Columbian day. We played it this way.

Two groomed stones would be chosen, one just large enough to fit comfortably in our hand. Each player took one such stone. In the center of play, a larger one was to be placed on that which our throw-stones were to rest if caught. A line some distance from said objects would be drawn from which our throw-stone was to be cast. The player known as *IT* would have his hand-stone on the carrying one below. As each player threw his own rock, his purpose was to dismount that stone resting on the base rock and to drive it as far from home as possible. This game we called frog-on-the-rock.

The hand rock being hit, or he who was called *IT*, was to recapture his own, replace the frog on the rock and tag the nearest rival. This done, he was to be *IT*. So we spent many an enjoyable hour in those playtime days with, perchance, the same amusement which brought many a similar tag on American soil five hundred or more years before Christopher Columbus looked into the eyes of San Salvador's red men.

Stilts

And again, what boy of my day never saw the ten foot tall giant trot around the circus ring at his county fair making fun for all? Was he not on stilts, clothed with foxy calicos? And how did he maintain balance on those long slim legs made of wood? Say what you will, Indian boys and girls, too, were thrilled during celebration times by this same monstrosity and even practiced the experience themselves, though it may have been on far cruder equipment.

And as for tops, they were almost as common for their times as were the Yo-Yos of today. Top spinning was common among the Eskimo of the far north in very early times. Their players tried to run around their igloos after throwing their tops and get back again while the top was still spinning. The Alaskan children, it is said, tried to see who could keep their tops erect and spinning longer than those of their competitors. The Oglala Sioux boy or girl flipped his top within a marked-off square. Those who succeeded, won. Those who failed, lost.

In certain cases the hand spindles and cords of the tops used, appear to have been related to spindles used in domestic weaving. At best, this was the conclusion of those who studied these matters. With the Zuñis, top-making

38

became a specialty. Their tops were marketed far and wide. In fact, Zuñi hands seem to have been uniquely skilled in this kind of work, especially in their doll or kachina making, as known in post-Columbian times.

Quoits and Popguns

Nor should we forget that youth of ancient times enjoyed the fun of quoits and popguns. There is a grain of exercise for those who enjoy such activities in these simple sports. With the American youth of ancient times, quoits were merely flattened objects made of wood or stone that were thrown toward an upright stick or stake. Should the disk strike the stake and lean there, the next player's purpose would be to dislodge it as we do today in playing quoits or in horseshoe pitching. And as for popguns, they of olden times knew how to use bean straws and sugar cane with their hollow interiors. In such they would put their small pellets of seeds or chewed dough and send these balls full force against the object selected. Even that, to them, gave real fun, as does shooting paper wads by our youth of today.

As for shuttlecock, it was also widely enjoyed. Both youths and their parents appear to have played at this pastime. It, like numerous amusements, stood near to the jovial hearts of the days of old. Shuttlecock of primitive American days, in form and practice, is much like our shuffleboard of today. Ours, of course, is played on smoothed, even-polished flooring. Theirs had to be on nature's own. But whoever the player, this type of innocent amusement yields its purposive results.

39

The Indian Bull-Roarer

Had you never seen an Indian bull-roarer, what on first sight would you have guessed it to look and sound like? Do you want me to tell you?

One evening, again at sundown, I happened into the ancient village of Zuñi, a pueblo community about eight hundred miles east from my home. The village seemed to be astir with life. Things were going wrong. Here and there could be seen gowned persons dodging in and out of doorways, apparently anxious about conditions as they were.

On inquiry I learned that Zuñi summer corn and family gardens had fallen victim to the grasshoppers. These flying pests filled the air by the millions, like the locust swarms of ancient Egypt in Moses' time. Fields that were green at sunrise, lay stripped by setting sun. You must possess a strong and virile imagination to visualize conditions as I saw them then and there.

The medicine men of old Zuñi had been in sitting in their council kiva for many hours about this matter. Could this scourge mean that an evil spirit was amongst them? Had some clan leader violated Zuñi's moral law? If so, who was it, and where could his image be found and exterminated: else might not all Zuñi infants and children perish from starvation and hunger as of ancient times?

The result was that witch doctors from a neighboring tribal group were called to Zuñi for counsel and help. They brought with them a bull-roarer. It was a simple but effective device, well calculated to challenge the souls of humans. On one end of a sturdy stick about a yard in length, tied with a strong yucca thong, was a hollow beam of like length. When whirled above the head, it yielded an unearthly roar. I have heard the deep cadence of the conch shell's call when used to alarm those in danger. Also I am still young enough to have heard the shocking sounds of those of the pioneer day called the horse fiddle. But to these, the Indian bull-roarer has little likeness.

As stated, I entered Zuñi at sundown. Quickly I found lodgment in the local trading post, operated by friendly hands. I bear witness to the fact that that first night was horrifying. So, too, was the second and the third. Then all was silence. Was the supposed witch found? That I do not know. But I do know that the Zuñi village was quiet again; and its people went to work like bees to recuperate their losses. This was my experience with the Indians' bull-roarer — an experience of which I want no more. Why it found placement as a minor *amusement* in our index is more than I know. I still question its placement there.

Cat's Cradle

Who has not enjoyed playing cat's cradle in the early evening hours by lamplight, when lights are dim and bedtime is nearing? With children of early years, its antics are fascinating.

As you know, the human fingers are the performers, the hand itself the stage. By putting the two hands together in the proper way and holding the two thumbs, you can throw the image of Peter Rabbit on the screen with perfect effect. There you can make him stand, wiggling his ears and dancing a jig like the real sport that he is. Or by a twist of your fingers you can imitate the baby in the bath tub, one of the more common of the charades of ancient China. Did our first Americans draw this amusing pastime from their far Asian home, or did they bring it

41

into being on early American soil? For this one, likewise, I have no answer; but in the rearing of my family of five, I have watched juveniles fascinated by it many times. We may be assured that it had its place among the amusements of our undated American homes, by the simple wickiups on our Pacific Rim, in the tepees of our prairies, or in the longhouses of the fearsome Iroquois peoples. It, too, was typically American, born and reared here, to the amusement of many of the days of yore, those of red man's past.

Red Man's Dexterity Games

W E NOW ENTER THE second phase of our primitive red man's gaming interests, those which have to do with his unique quickness, both in body and mind, fit aptitudes for his survival in his friendly, yet unfriendly world of nature. Like all primitive men, his world was filled with hazards and dangers of many kinds. It was for him to meet the threat of life or death when it came and as he found it. So it is with all.

Do not risk and danger lie at the center of all living? Has not the red man's upward climb paralleled that of all humanity for unnumbered centuries? In gaining his food, shelter, and body comforts what more could have been

43

expected from America's static abundance at the hands of their leaders and wise men, as with simple march they moved southward from the cold, cold north, the Bering Strait of our present Alaska?

A book titled *The Ghost of Kingikty,* just off the press, came to my desk only yesterday. Its author is an Eskimo fullblood, proud of her ancestral line. Schooled in the traditions of her people, she writes thus, if we would know their ways.

> On the mountain side of the village there lived a young chief named Soukee. Just recently his wife had given him a son. One day when he and his hunting crew made ready to go out to sea a sudden squall had come up and prevented them from going out to the ice flows. So he and his crew went up the slope of the mountain to play 'kick the ball'. . . .[10]

and so on and so on.

Was this the "foot-cast ball" game mentioned in our list of dexterity sports, known to primeval Americans? Or could it have been a singular traditional game known only to the Eskimo people as such? We wonder! This much we know, there are artifacts of ideas as well as artifacts of things. As often said, the thought of a thing comes before its actual creation, and this too is true. Perchance, the Eskimo game of "kick the ball" was unique and singular to their culture. The point is that a ball game of some kind was implied, and its mention was in connection with their fables and legends.

But not so with the "foot-cast ball" game cited in the index of our Indian games of dexterity. True, there are only three known continental areas where this game was cited. These were among the Meriposan stock and the Apache people of California, far removed from Alaska,

44

and the ancient Zuñians of our mountain country to the east.

In describing this game, one of its observers states that the ball used was a stone, about three inches in diameter. This would be placed in the upper side of the player's toes on the right foot and thrown as far as possible toward an established goal; he who outdistanced his rivals won. This was the way they played their "foot-cast ball" in the ancient time. Simple, wasn't it?

Archery

Only those who have carefully examined the red man's bow and arrow of prehistorical time, as artifacts stored away, can understand the scrupulous care spent by their makers in their construction.

First of all, to be effective, the arrow shaft must be straight and strong, else their intended route of travel may miss their mark. Next, its bow timber likewise must have elasticity and driving power. Both must carry enduring qualities. To meet shifting winds, moreover, the arrow shaft at its power-end must be steadied by feather guides, suited to the need. And at the alternate end of the shaft it must carry its deadly arrow, fixed firmly in the shaft's end.

Its killing tip may be held in place by finely cut thongs of tough leather, the work of skilled hands. This is the red man's bow and arrow, his defense and attack medium, his sole means of safety, other than his own arms and legs. Perhaps his atlatl and dart,[11] similar in a way to the javelin of the early Greeks and Romans, may have preceded the universal bow and arrow later known to America's red men. It was a straight shaft, linked by a sling-like thong held in the hand of its user. It was thrown by muscle power alone, in its primitive day.

45

But since that time, what strides scientific archery has made! Today, as all know, it has become one of the most valued dexterity builders known to modern life. Instruction in archery is now offered through many channels. Our high schools and colleges provide for just such training. A visit to any up-to-date sports shop tells the same story. Eyesight, steadiness of hand, quick thought perception and action are its major products. Hence for the age that lies ahead, archery must be one of the red man's most prized gifts to America's future.

Shinney

Shinney was a favored game with America's red men long before they met the whites, migrants from across the eastern seas. With them, in contrast to foot-cast ball, just described, shinney in prehistoric times was played by America's primitives continent-wide.

The tools used were about what they are today, especially among the children of my boyhood day who lived in rural districts. First, there was some kind of a ball to be hit. This might be a stone, a tin can, a block of cast-off wood, a leather bag if available, or just anything to take the swats. And as for the shinney stick with us, of course, it was home grown, and with our jackknives whittled into shape as conditions demanded.

Shinney with the American Indians was not a summertime sport alone. When their streams and lakes froze over, these offered a splendid area for a field of play.

Dr. J. W. Hudson describes this sport thus as played by certain of the California Indians. Says he, their clubs were made of "mountain mahogany" and their *o-lo-las*, "shinney balls" were carved carefully out of the same material.

46

Moreover, two or more men played in "couples or pairs" from a starting line. The captains at station first strike their respective balls toward their partners. If the ball falls short of this, it must be returned to its official for another throw. The last stationed partner must get it, the ball, across the goal line to count as score. Station-keepers must stay within their own territories or be penalized.

This description rings a bell with us today. Where shinney is still played, it is much the same as that which amused and entertained the red men and their families of the ancient days. And what about modern hockey, does it not spring from the same virgin roots? I wonder!

Hoop and Pole Game

When I first saw this title, my mind jumped to our Maypole activities of my collegiate day. Of course, this was its story. A May Day queen was chosen. Then a pole, perhaps ten or more feet high, was brought to the campus. Strips of colored cotton cloth were selected twenty or more feet in length, these to be wound about the Maypole in colorful fashion to the sound of dance music.

Incidentally, one day I asked my wife who had spent twenty years or more in distant West China, whether its boys and girls had a similar festivity. Her answer was no. Our practice had not reached that far west, she explained. But the Indians' sport, their hoop and pole game, yields strong likelihood of its having come from the northwest, even from across the Bering Strait so ancient and almost universal was its practice among our indigenous red men. This sport, enjoyed by this vigorous and dexterity-loving people, in general, was played in this way.

A field of play would be selected, about fifty or more feet in length. Lanes would be cleared in this field of all obstructions, such as weeds or brushwood, to be followed with the leveling of certain paths on the ground, a foot or so wide, over which the hoop, a circular instrument was to roll.

This done, the contestants appeared with their poles, eight to ten feet in length, something like the chivalric European knights of old. In hand, of course, was their choice magic ring, perhaps two feet, more or less, in diameter, toward which they would throw their spear or pole. The charmed ring would be netted, something like today's basketball basket. The number of such meshes, their size, color, and kind were decisive factors. The object of the thrower was to pin his hoop to the ground at a favored distance from its starting line. The score earned was determined by the number of pole-throws required, and the hoop meshes pierced.

What rivalries this simple sport engendered among those of the long ago! As for the Plains peoples, James Adair, of whom we shall know more a bit later, left this record, describing a hoop and pole contest among Choctaw peoples of old Mississippi. Said he:

> The warriors have another favorite game called *chungke* . . . which may be called "running hard labor". They have near their statehouse a square piece of ground well cleaned . . . Only one or two on a side play at this ancient game.
> They have a stone about 2 fingers broad at the edge, and 2 spans round: Each party has a pole about 8 feet long, smooth, and tapering at each end, the points flat. They set off abreast of each other at 6 yards from the end of the playground: then one of them hurls the stone on its edge, in as direct a line as he can . . . toward the middle of the other end of the

square. When they have run a few yards, each darts his pole . . . as near as he can guess . . . close to the stone. . . . When this is the case the person counts 2 of the game . . . [12]

and the game thus goes on until an agreed upon total in scores has been reached. This for the Choctaws was one of their favorite games during winter months before the buffalo began their roaming.

We could continue almost endlessly the digging up of such descriptions of our early red men's games of dexterity; but perhaps enough has been said to lure some to their further study. Should this be the case, perhaps at least one of our purposes will have been accomplished. However, the activities ahead are just as alluring. This involves what came to light with the researches of our body of government specialists who opened the doorway to the study. It was, not alone the amusement activities and the dexterity interests of America's pre-Columbian natives, but also their games of chance which were well suited to their precarious mode of life. These are to be our next area of exploitation. We trust that the artifacts, tangible and intangible, yet to be brought to light, may be of interest and value to all who pursue our quest to its end.

Indian Risk and
Games of Chance

WITHOUT A GRAIN of egotism, let me share my life's interests with the reading public. From early childhood sports of many kinds have been my main interest in living.

At age five I was peeking through the knot holes of the Cincinnati Reds' board fence which debarred me from their field of play. As time went on I fished in the Ohio River, and as a growing boy hunted over the neighboring countryside, rife with American Indian tradition and earlier occupation. During this same juvenile period I sold

51

newspapers, played kid baseball, football, shinney, and the numerous games well known to that age group.

In college I earned my baseball and football letters and was proud to wear them. In addition to my class work and study, I took part in glee club activities and debate, along with the many social functions which filled the hours.

Then on a shoe string — as some would say, I crossed the broad Atlantic in a cattle boat, earning my way by feeding and watering hundreds and hundreds of Texas Longhorns, much to my own interest and peril. While in Britain I watched the English game of football, there called rugby, as played at Eton and Rugby schools. Too, on the Thames River I saw the long slim skiffs, called shells, of Oxford and Cambridge universities in their rivalry as, like Indian canoes, they skimmed over the water like fleet butterflies.

Then, again, it was back home and to America's wilds. Soon my wanderlust led me to Florida. In its quiet Everglades I fished and hunted crocodiles. Next, fortune called me to the state of Maine and its almost limitless forests, the home of innumerable deer, bears, and kindred forms of American wildlife. Then came my mid-west, then my Rocky Mountain west, and finally my Pacific far west, with many trips back and forth as the years have come and gone. This, in a nut shell, has been my experience. This has been my life's story.

Recently one of my daughters was in the desert lands of western Arizona. While traveling one of its ghost towns on the search for artifacts, she and her husband met a young Indian. His home was in certain nearby caves. He said he lived on rattlesnake meat as his major diet. But someone had relieved him of his supply of that delicacy, so he was out hunting rabbits. All that he had in hand were his trusted homemade bow and arrows as hunting instruments. And why? He said he refused to carry a gun

52

and powder shells. These were white men's killers. He preferred to live life like his ancestors amidst nature's plenty. Perhaps this is enough about life's way. Let us get on with the red man's risk games and his games of chance, lest we lose our way.

Measuring the
Red Man's I.Q.

CHANCE GAMES, says one authority, offers our best instrument known for the measuring of the red man's I.Q., as well as that of any other primitive racial group. If this type of sportsmanship is helpful in determining the present Indian's power to think, as well as his ability to adjust to changing life, why should not the same technique, carefully studied, serve as an eye-opener as to why he did what he did as he did it and what with him were the results. At least this suggestion supplies us with a beginning for the work at hand.

55

But first let us be clear in our definitions. What do we mean by the term *chance*, especially if we give it the gambling bent which is frequently done? And what do we mean by the term *guessing*, as used in the document studied? These inquiries may appear to be extraneous or beside the purpose of our investigations: but are they?

In a sense, is not the whole of life based on chance? We are told that we come into life naked and we go out naked. Based on the devastating power of modern nuclear science, has history or pre-history ever had a period when the fate of mankind was less certain? One blast from the skies above or from tunnels beneath, in the bat of an eye, can blow humanity into eternity. In the light of these terms, is not all of life a gamble?

In our approach to this issue we need to be united on the red man's unique philosophy, or what we should call his outlook on life. Indeed, he was an animist, with all of this that his age-old religious training gave. He looked to the skies for his gods, and he little questioned the authority of his medicine men. His clouds were filled with spirits of every kind, and to him what they willed was right. Hence, when he bet on a game, the result of his action was to him law. We have canvassed this concept before, but it is well to review it now. It was the red man's way of life. He lived and acted unhesitatingly under this concept of life, backed with a wealth of ritualism and unreasoned action which made him what he was in action.

While the number of games mentioned in our index are few, their purport is not to be undervalued. The writers give more space to them than to all others. Few though they be, only five in all, they mark out the crux of continental thought-life for the red men of America.

Dice Games

THE NUMBER OF dice games played by our first Americans were almost beyond count. They were played everywhere. It was their major type of self expression for youth as well as for adults. They saw no sin in taking a chance. Again, the results were the will of their gods.

For ages, dice of one kind and another have been used in the playing of games. It was so with the Greeks and the Romans, and it was so with our pre-Columbian Americans. In current life, dice are cubical in shape, each of their six faces carrying a number varying from one to six, usually in dot form. Moreover, they are operated in sets of two. On their throw, if one die comes up carrying one dot, it goes for one for the count. If the other yields a six, their total amounts to seven in all, which is counted as the lucky number. So the game progresses till a predetermined sum is reached which marks the winner of the game.

Indian dice of the early day were made in great variety, both in size, shape, and kind. Some were of stone, others of hardened wood, some were of animal bones — those of the walrus, the buffalo, or the caribou. Likewise grains of maize were used by some, as were plum seeds, acorns, and many other objects close at hand.

At such games usually there were judges — the tribal chief, the clan shaman, the medicine man, respected by all — to preside and keep order when feeling ran high. However, these contests usually were orderly and of a friendly nature, played in the atmosphere of neighbors and friends, subject to the will of the fates.

Women Take a Hand

For a century or more, Monte Carlo, on the warm shores of southern France, has been the professional gaming center of our modern world. Day and night its fortune wheels spin and its dice are thrown, leaving some rich, others poor, according to the unwritten laws of chance. There empires and crowns have been won or lost according to the way chance worked. So, too, on the floor of New York City's stock exchange we can see this same mania at work. What has been called financial bidding there has been professionalized. But if you would see America's primitive womanhood engaged in this chance activity you will have to go elsewhere. So to the wild White Mountains of Arizona let us trek to watch a women's dice game as described by an eye witness. Here, in part, is a copy of

58

his report. Remember, this is the land of Geronimo, the red man's master risk-taker!

"This is a women's game," says our guide, "and is played with great ardor. The staves are three in number, from 8 to 10 inches long and flat on one side.

"The playground is circular . . . about 5 feet in diameter. The center of this circle is formed by a flat rock of any convenient size, generally from 8 to 10 inches in diameter. On the circumference forty stones are arranged in sets of ten, to be used as counters. Not less than two or more than four can participate in the game at one time," though others, unnumbered are apt to be onlookers, says our leader.

"In playing," our informant continues, "the sticks are grasped in the hand and thrown on end upon the rock in the center with force enough to make them rebound. As they fall, flat or round face upward, the throw amounts to 1 or 10. . . . Should one of the players, in making her count, continue from her set of counters to the adjoining set of her opponent's and strike the place marked by the opponent's tally marker, it throws the opponent's count out of the game, and she must start anew."[13]

This description sounds simple, doesn't it? And so it is. But to the players it means winning or losing, even to the point of losing the very clothing on one's back.

While these matters of our aboriginal American dice throwing are fresh in mind, let us inquire as to how extensive, continent-wide, this practice among the Amerindians may have been. On this point our text says this: "A game or games of this type here described" were "existing among 130 tribes belonging to 30 linguistic stocks, and from no one tribe does it appear absent." In other words, dice gaming was almost, if not entirely, a universal sport with our first Americans of pre-Columbian times.

59

Native American
Stick Games

WHAT THUS FAR has been said about American Indian dice gaming could be repeated with emphasis about the red man's many stick games. A frank personal confession is due at this point. For years I was, indeed, puzzled about the place of *sticks* in the Indian's mode of thought. Personally, I have seen many such artifacts in the caves, the shrines, and the kivas of the up-country of our great Southwest. Desert places seem to be full of them. But what did they mean? Why were they there? Why did the natives place so much importance upon such common objects?

61

I was reared in a much simpler religious atmosphere than this. I believed in a God above, and of a divine personal Jesus, thought to be with me and within me, everywhere and at all times. But what about the miraculous, the superhuman, the magical, the wonder-working power of these sticks? This, indeed, was a puzzle to me. And it was not until I centered thought on the Indians' intimacy with nature that I understood. My Thunder Mountain experience at sunset, earlier cited, was fundamental to this transition.

Sufficient to say, the number and kind of red man's sanctified sticks are almost infinite in number. They are like the leaves of nature's trees or the blades of grass of the fields, they are beyond count. Wherever he set foot, they are to be found.

However, the genius of his functional hands and the mood of his mind and spirit determines their use and working power. Dedicated to his deities, they become his wonder workers. To him their powers are real. Hence, whatever else, it is so.

Can you imagine a bundle of sticks, any number of dry sticks, painted or unpainted, carved or uncarved, as carrying mesmeric or hypnotic powers? To visualize these, you need to see only two such artifacts. One might be arrow shafts, painted with varying designs, used by our many groups of native red men of the long ago. The second form of Indian gaming sticks could be flat or processed disks bearing many carved images of deceased persons of the past, gifted with powers and abilities of persuasion desired by those alive. In such relics the finite and the infinite join. At least this seems to be the concept of those who worked through such shafts in their stick guessing games. Now for a few examples. This one springs to mind. It comes from the Three Rivers country, near Quebec,

Canada. It is brief and easily understood. Says its giver:

> The game of straw (paille) is played with little straws made for this purpose and which are divided very unequally into three parts as in hazard. Our Frenchmen have not as yet been able to learn this game. It is full of vivacy; and straws are among them what cards are with us.[14]

Our second is a bit more complete, played among the Miami peoples, who lived in the vicinity of the St. Joseph River region, now Michigan, and observed by a French missionary, P. de Charlevoix, who wrote:

> That day the Pottawatomi had come to play the game of straws with the Miami. They played in the hut of the chief, and in a place opposite. These straws are small, about as thick as a wheat straw and 2 inches long. Each player takes a bundle of them, usually containing two hundred and one, always an uneven number.
>
> After having well shaken them about, making meaningful a thousand contortions and invoking the spirits, they separate them, with a sort of thorn or pointed bone, into parcels of ten. Each one takes his own, haphazard, and he who has chosen the parcel containing eleven wins a certain number of points, as may have been agreed upon. The game is 60 or 80. . . . They also told me that there is as much skill as chance in this game, and that the savages are extremely clever at it, as at all other games; that they give themselves up to it and spend whole days and nights at it; that sometimes they do not stop playing until they are entirely naked, having no more to lose.[15]

This report confirms the legend now to be released: believed or not believed, as you may think best. It comes to us from the British Columbia region and was believed by its oldest of its very old.

63

The Indian Legend of Sticks

A young man was very fond of playing *atlih* (Indian sticks), so fond that he could scarcely control his passion for its play. So far did he go one time in its playing that first he was stripped of his valuables — his bow, his arrows, his tomahawk, his blanket, even the clothes on his back. Hence, naked he played on. Then his wager included his children, his wife, his parents.

Disgusted with his conduct, his fellow villagers turned away from him. They moved to another spot in their forests. They also took with them all of their belongings. They extinguished the fires in every lodge so that he might perish. This they did in disgust, yet he played on with his unknown guest-gambler.

Of course without fire he could not live, nor could he take it with him. Soon he was almost frozen, dying from hunger. Suddenly he caught sight of smoke in a tall spruce tree close by. Thought he, "where there is smoke, there is fire. I shall investigate." Naked and cold, he followed the glimmering spark.

Soon he saw sparks flying. In his dream he came upon a great lodge, covered with branches of pine cones and conifers. He peeked through a chink in its siding. Alone, there sat an old man close to two large fires burning in the lodge.

Aware of the young gambler's presence, the old man said, "Come in, my son-in-law, what are you doing out there in the cold?" Like Milton's Paradise Lost, stripped of all of his possessions, even his parents, wife, and children, even his aspiration, the young man entered, hoping to go to the great beyond. In fact this old man was none other than *Yihta*, the spirit of gaming itself.

"Son-in-law," he said, "you seem alone in these forests. Where have you been? What have you done? Have you been gambling?" "Yes," replied the young man. "I have gambled and lost all."

Then the old man turned a bit. There stood his daughter, a woman of charm and beauty. To her the old man said, "For this youth roast a deer's haunch. Cook it good and long. He is cold, hungry, discouraged, but brave. Treat him well!" This she did. While the maiden moved with dignity, the youth wondered.

Meanwhile, with a long, slim gambling stick the old man dug a deep hole in the hot embers before him. Then he called to the youth. Said he, "Put this arrow to your lips! Suck it! Suck its grease, son-in-law! Gamble where you will, you shall win. Then come back to this long-house. My daughter shall be your wife."

The young man went forth. He gambled. He won. The maiden whom he had met was his wife in disguise. His children, his parents, all that he had lost was recovered.[16]

This is the legend of the Indians' gambling sticks as of days of yore. Many who carry aboriginal red skins today, sons of those long gone, bask in the shadow of its potency and believe it in their inward parts as they do many of nature's mysteries about them on every hand. For an age such as ours, such confidence in the unseen is invaluable. Let fictitious sorcery be suppressed; but to keep faith in the Great Spirit, the Great Holy, is the back bone of the red man's traditional outlook on life. As a working policy it seems invaluable in meeting the uncertainties of every pressing current hour. To this conclusion modern science drives us. Toward this end without disdain, let our aboriginal peoples lead the way.

Indians! Play Ball!

IN MANY PARTS of North America, in as many different languages unknown to European ears, this call "INDIANS! PLAY BALL," could have been heard long, long before the Pilgrim Fathers first set foot on New World soil. And what was more, Indian ball games were of as many kinds and natures, much like those who played them. But toward the pre-Columbian era one such game was known far and wide among America's red men. For the want of a better description the French who entered present eastern Canada called it La Crosse. Just why this name, I do not know. But that it was played in one form and another from the Atlantic to the Pacific coast seems clear, judging from the artifacts left behind.

67

In nature, La Crosse, in European eyes, later appeared to be a composite of what today we say is our football, baseball, lawn tennis, basketball, and even hockey, if not others. Moreover, in play it was a husky game, played with vigor and vim; played as only America's red men could play. James Adair, the British pack peddler, born to European ways and located in what today is our sunny South, thus describes what he saw in our south land.

James Adair Sees Indians Play Ball

And by the way, do you want to know who this James Adair was? He, too, wrote a book titled *A History of the American Indians*. Have you read it? I have. It was published, hardback, in London, in 1775, no copyright. To do its work, of course, he had to bring all of his writing materials with him — his paper, his pen-quills, his ink, even his trader's pack in which he carried his merchandise to be marketed to native Americans, men, women, and children.

At odd hours, in America's wilds, Adair wrote about what he experienced and saw. For example: The Indians watched his fingers as he wrote. They were curious. What did those scratches mean? Some were so suspicious that thinking them connected in some way with dreaded witchcraft, perhaps, they took his paper and spirited it away. And remember: to get more from far away England would require months of time, together with added expense. But, thank fortune, Adair persisted and today we can read about what he saw. This is it.

Adair says that this game was, indeed, one of severe exercise. To his mind, it was well calculated to develop the dexterity of muscle and mind so much needed by the natives in this wild land. The ball used, he tells us, "is made of a piece of scraped deer's skin, moistened and

68

stuffed hard with deer's hair." Its cover, moreover, was "strongly sewed with deer's sinews," much as are our baseballs of today. These balls, he says, were about two inches in diameter like our baseballs and suited to the work at hand.

Ball sticks, comparable to our ball bats, likewise were used for getting this object to its goal. In length these were about two or more feet long, made of the sturdiest material and frequently ornamented with family carvings which were as strange in their meaning to Adair as were his written words to them. Now for Adair's description direct. Says he:

> Ball playing is their chief and most favorite game; and it is such severe exercise, as to show it was originally calculated for a hardy and expert race of people like themselves, and the ancient Spartans.
>
> In the net at the ends of their bats they catch the ball and throw it a great distance, when not prevented by some of the opposite party, who try to intercept them.
>
> The goal is about 500 yards in length: at each end of it, they fix two long bending poles into the ground, 3 yards apart below, but slanting a considerable way outward. The party who happens to throw the ball over these counts 1; but if it be thrown underneath, it is cast back, and played for as usual.
>
> The gamesters are equal in number on each side; and at the beginning of every course of the ball they throw it up high in the center of the ground, and in a direct line between the two goals.
>
> When the crowd of players prevents the one who catched the ball from throwing it off with a long direction, he commonly sends it in the right course by an artful sharp twirl. They are so exceedingly expert in this manly exercise, that, between the goals, the ball is mostly flying the different ways, by the force of the playing sticks, without falling to the ground, for they are not allowed to catch it with their hands.
>
> It is surprising to see how swiftly they fly, when

closely chased by a nimble-footed pursuer; when they are intercepted by one of the opposite party, his fear of being cut by the ball sticks commonly gives them an opportunity of throwing it perhaps a hundred yards; but the antagonist sometimes runs up behind, and by a sudden stroke dashes down the ball.

It is a very unusual thing to see them act spitefully in any sort of game, not even in this severe and tempting exercise.[17]

Thanks, Friend Adair, this description, penned nearly 200 years ago, sounds much like those now heard daily over the air. Now we can quite understand the vim and pep which the youth of America's yesterday put into their playlife. Having lived among them as their pack trader, we trust that you experienced no further inconvenience in your writing or marketing of your English merchandise — your mirrors, your shaving sticks, your face powders, your glass beads, in exchange for their furs, their spices, their curiously designed floor mats, their tobacco — things coveted even today by all Britishers overseas. Indeed, with you friend Adair, we have lived those days over again, far though we feel in time and space from those ancient days of yore.

George Catlin Sees La Crosse

About a century after Adair's time, George Catlin, the noted artist on American Indian life, likewise saw this same game as played by the Choctaw peoples, then dwellers in Indian territory, now Oklahoma. By way of introduction, he states that it was "no uncommon occurence for six or eight hundred or a thousand of these young men to engage in a game of ball, with five or six times that number of men, women, and children looking on." For they, too, enjoyed these sports, in contrast to the daily routine of life.

70

Artist Catlin left us this satisfying word picture of what he saw on America's southern prairies. We have his word for this:

Monday afternoon at 3 o'clock, I rode out . . . to a very pretty prairie . . . to the ball-play-ground of the Choctaws where we found several thousand Indians encamped. There were two points of timber, about half a mile apart, in which the two parties for the play . . . were encamped; and laying between them, the prairie on which the game was to be played. . . .

During the afternoon, we loitered about among the different tents . . . of the two encampments, and . . . at sundown witnessed the ceremony of measuring out the ground . . . or goals which were to guide the play.

This game had been arranged and "made up" three or four months before the parties met to play it, and in the following manner: The two champions who led the two parties . . . send runners, with the ball-sticks . . . to be touched by each of the chosen players. . . . But soon after dark a procession of lighted flambeaux was seen coming from each encampment . . . and at the beat of the drums and chants of the women each party of players commenced the "ball-play" dance. . . .

In this game each player was dressed alike, that is, divested of all dress, except the girdle . . . ; and in these desperate struggles for the ball, when it is up, where hundreds are running together and leaping, . . . tripping and throwing, . . . every voice raised to the highest key . . . there are rapid successions of feats, and of incidents, that astonish and amuse far beyond the conception of anyone . . .

Each time that the ball was passed between the stakes of either party, one was counted for their game . . . when it was again started by the judges of the play, and a similar struggle ensued, and so on until the successful party arrived to 100.[18]

71

That, of course, was the end of the game, except for the celebrations, perhaps for days, thereafter. This was what this artist of refined inclinations experienced as he saw America's red men at what at that time was by them called play.

Off to the Foot Races

ATTENTION EARLIER has been called to the foot placement of our aboriginals from early childhood. From coast to coast, with our red men, this practice amounted almost to an obsession. With youth and adulthood of both sexes it blossomed out into the practice of foot racing, a body builder of the first importance.

With the Indians the long trails which stretched across the American continent told their own story. Should you have desired, before the first whites appeared you could have traveled, foot-wise, as you know, over the red man's Great War Path from Maine to Florida's Everglades in times of peace over such a trail in comfort, though not by automobile. Or, if from east to west was your desire, you could have started on the Atlantic rim via The Wilderness Road, a marvelous Indian trail, and traveled continuously by way of the old Natchez Trail, to the Mississippi, thence across the prairies to the present Pueblo village of Taos; next by the ancient Zuñi Trail to today's San Diego with slight inconvenience, other than the strain of light-foot travel.

This fact led the Iroquois people to specialize in foot racing in its many forms. So, too, with their neighbors, the Cherokee, and other aboriginal groups along the way. At times rivalry in the fine art of running became intense among America's primevals, west as well as east.

Among the Navajo their tribal shamen constantly were on the lookout for young men with nimble limbs and deep chest power. Their hero was he who could win for them the foot races of the mountains. Foot racing, we are told, was their specialty before the appearance of the white man's horse. Their territories comprised open desert country from horizon to horizon. Hence they loved to run.

In such a contest the Navajo runner jibed his rival with a squawk-like signal. It sounded something like this, we are told: *Ooh, Ooh, Ooh*. It was boastful in its spirit, much like the call to combat heard during European medieval days when one knight challenged another to clash of arms. If accepted, the challenger then put two fingers together which simply meant "get set." Then the race was on.

But there is more to this tale. Should the Navajo win, he whipped his opponent across the back with a yucca scourge in utter disdain. Should he lose, the challenger urged his sponsor to "lay it on," meaning not to take it easy, for defeat with them called for just such treatment.

74

A Short Mandan Run

Now for the story of a *short* Mandan run in the North Dakota country, described as Olympic in character. Professor F. Y. Hayden here tells us what he saw so late as the year 1862. A century or more ago, foot races in our great West among these red men are known to have had a span of twenty miles, or more, like the historic Marathon of ancient Greece, but completed in less than four hours' time.

The following is the account of a nine mile race watched by Professor Hayden.

A race course of 3 miles on the level prairie was laid off, cleared of every obstruction, and kept in order for the expressed purpose. Posts were planted to mark the initial and terminating points, and over the track the young men tested the elasticity of their limbs during the fine summer and autumn months. . . .

Six pairs of runners whose bets have been matched now start to run the 3 mile course, which is to be repeated three times before it can be decided. . . .
The runners are entirely naked, except their moccasins, and their bodies are painted in various ways from head to foot.

The first set having accomplished about half the first course, as many more are started, and this is continued as long as any competitors remain, until the entire track is covered with runners. . . .

And the judges award the victory to those who come out, by handing each a feather painted red, the first six winning the prize. These, on presenting the feathers to the judges at the starting-point, are handed the property staked against their own.[19]

The first and second feats here mentioned, says our informant, "are seldom strongly contested." But the third is what counts. Can the runner stick it out? Does he have what it takes to run nine miles? In the final stretch, continues the writer, "every nerve is strained," the spectators are excited to passion, and yells and gestures that defy description are to be experienced on every hand. Those who have shown fleetness and powers of endurance, but who are not winners, are praised by the tribal public crier, and many are showered with acclaim for days thereafter. Yes, at least throughout the West such foot races were commonplace, each adapted to local needs. What wonder, then, that in current times, like talent on the part of present Indian youth, red men's names, usually in Anglicized form, often appear in today's halls of fame? And one thing more should be mentioned in this same connection, namely, seldom are such awards issued to those who act with rashness, and seldom does ill health attend their way.

Young Play with Old

A GAIN, EARLY IN AUGUST, my feet moved toward
Zuñi village, New Mexico, but under conditions very
different than those which took me there at the time
of the grasshopper swarms and the sounds of the hideous
bull-roarer. College duties were over and I was ready for
fun.

Shortly before my arrival, upper Zuñi River valley
had had one of its typical cloud bursts. Just preceding it,
the river bed was as dry as desert sands can well be. But
upon my appearance, its banks were flowing full. Cut off
from my usual trading post quarters, I sat feet stripped,
dangling them in liquid gold.

A middle-aged woman came by. Cautiously I spoke to her and said: "Madam! Did you ever hear the name Matilda Coxe Stevenson?" A surprised look came over her face. With vim she responded: "She, probably, was the first white woman to ever enter our village. She was here three generations ago. She nursed my great-grandmother through a death struggle with pneumonia and won. She, too, was a gatherer of old Indian relics." She was right. Sufficient to say, the skies quickly cleared and Zuñi went on with its festival of August fun for which I had come.

Early the next morning at sunrise the voice of Zuñi's head priest sounded forth loud and clear. All were called, both young and old, to commemorate their age-old get-together in the village plaza, their fun-for-all day. Harvests had been gathered. Rain had come; and all were to be true to the gods. And it was so.

By nine o'clock that morning Zuñi's drums began to beat. In response, within the hour the walls of nearby solid homes were responding. I verify this statement, for my back was pressed against them. Tier upon tier of receding housetops were crowded with watchers, splendid viewpoints, women and children, dressed in their gaudiest. If I ever saw a superb combination of nature's rainbow colors, it was then. Colorful skirts, shawls, together with headgear of astonishing beauty glittered from every corner. Thanks to fortune I, too, was there!

Zuñi's day of fun was on. A body of agile youth assembled in its plaza, may we call it Zuñi's Central Park for comparative purpose. With that freedom, common to this wide open country, all seemed to be fully in the play mood. Some played with throw darts, bound together with corn husks, similar to those used in the aboriginal ring-pole game earlier described. Others spun tops of curious design, with a skill which challenged attention. Still others danced

78

about on homemade stilts, seemingly innocent of all that was going on about them. Several were mimicking the turkey trot, the buzzard's flight, even the mystical giant's stride of the nearby Thunder Mountain.

From hidden quarters, the judges of this climaxing celebration came into this busy arena. With clear voice they announced that the traditional relay race was to begin.

A group of teen-age boys first lined up. For this purpose moccasin scratches were made in the dust for the rivals at rightful places in the plaza. Then appeared a like number of girls as opponents, giggling and laughing. With what skill and enthusiasm both strove for the honors of the day!

On the call of the master judge, a leader from each side leaped forth. With his racing stick held in one hand, like a flash of lightning he leaped toward his teammates at the opposite side of the plaza. So swift were his movements that a trail of dust was left behind him. With outstretched arm that stick was held toward his companion, bound by the watchful eye of the race judge not to move till reached by said stick. Then off he went like a flash of lightning. With what skill and enthusiasm both boys and girls, in their own marked off territory, each pressed for the prize, urged on by those who cheered them from their home housetops. That scene matched anything that it has been mine to witness anywhere. Yells filled the air by rival supporters, both young and old.

Finally, Zuñi's old men took their part in this relay race, though, of course, theirs was only for them. But did they enjoy it! Some clearly were in their dotage. However, age did not matter. For them it was fun-day, too. To wind things up toward sundown, Zuñi's town clowns appeared. Naturally, they were in the most grotesque costumes, designed for the same fun purposes. They frolicked about like ghosts of time long gone by.

79

For one day, at least, hazards of insect pests, dangers of drought and flood, fears of invading enemies, and the perils of disease and sorrow were forgotten by these Zuñi dwellers. All the world, including the whites, were their friends. What a day! Such scenes defy description. But for one fact I was thankful. I was there. I saw old Zuñi, ancient though it is, and was, at play. On that day I revised my image of the red man in general. He is a human. He loves life. And he knows how to play.

Tom-Toms and Indian Voices

An Indian Choral Group in Maine

IN MY BOYHOOD DAYS I carried the common concept of American Indian life, as earlier stated. His
image was that of a wild man, a silent individual, given
to few words, but daring deeds. To me he had no songs of
beauty, no emotions of love nor tender feelings toward
others. His brow was knit, his soul, if he had one, was
shrunken, his voice was stilled in evil meditation. He

81

was an evil worker, a trouble maker. To me, again, that was his image.

Somewhere in the rugged state of Maine, close to where I trace my branch of the Jones family, I picked up a shattered old pamphlet of questionable age. Its title page had been torn away; it gave no date of its printing; apparently it was, indeed, old. Today it lies in the archives of Colby College Library, one of the many artifacts that have crossed my pathway with the passing of the moons and winters.

In a nutshell that pamphlet carried the story of a little frontier chapel on America's early exploratory day, long before the coming of modern Maine. The builder of that chapel was a member of a monastic order from France, proud of his Christian heritage. He came to America's shores to convert the native Indians to the Christian way of life, as formalized by the church. In doing so, he needed those who could sing. May we let his quote tell its own story. Said he in that shattered pamphlet:

> The [Indian] village in which I live is called *Nanrantsouak* [now known as Norridgewock], and is situated on the banks of a river [the Kennebec] which empties into the sea. . . . I have erected a Church there, which is neat and elegantly ornamented.
>
> I have indeed, thought it my duty to spare nothing either in the decoration of the building itself, or the beauty of those articles which are used in our holy ceremonies. . . .
>
> I have also formed a little choir of about forty young Indians, who assist in Divine Service in cassacks and surplices. They have each their own appropriate functions as much to serve in the Holy Sacrifice of the Mass, as to chant the Divine Offices of the consecration."

So these native Eastern youths responded to the tutelage of Father Rasles and his priestly yearnings in a fashion which pleased not only him but also their immediate relatives, for the record concludes with these words: "for the processions which they make with the crowds of Indians, who often come from a long distance to engage in these exercises, and you will be edified by the beautiful order they observe, and the devotion they show."[20]

A West Coast Revelation

A short time ago, a research volume of modest size came into my hand which was shocking in its convincement. Earlier I had been prepared to yield mental assent to the fact that our pre-Columbian natives had a rich lore of musical ability, somewhat akin to their leaning for folklore and homely home-fire folk stories. But until faced with the facts, I was unaware of the almost universal passion of our aboriginal Americans for folk songs and folk music which touched almost every element of their being.

However, this came with a recent research publication titled *Nootka and Quileute Music*,[21] published by our U. S. Bureau Of American Ethnology, in 1939. Its author spent many years at its compilation, leaving no stone unturned as a scholar in his search for the truth of the thesis carried.

Briefly, the Quileute people about whom he wrote lived on our west coast on Vancouver Island, a jut of land which projects out into the peaceful Pacific Ocean, far, far from Maine's woodlands just cited.

The peoples mentioned called themselves not Indians but *Kwe-not-che-chat*, which to them merely meant "the people who live on a point of land projecting into the sea," or something to that effect. As studied, the music of these red men of the west typified that of red men, continent-wide, for ages uncounted. Had you read Dr.

83

A. L. Kroeber's amusing story, "Two Mohave Brothers — One Wife" embedded in our publication *So Say the Indians*, we would appreciate the assertion that as a race, red men almost universally are a singing people. Almost every thing they do, ceremonially and otherwise, has its melody to which it is sung. Hence they are a *singing people*.

The Quileute publication just cited classified the songs mentioned into no less than twenty-five or more singular groups, according to their content and purpose. One of these is a set of six songs dedicated to their interest in timely whaling, one of the major sources of their livelihood. Another is their so-called potlatch songs having to do with their canoeing and seagoing ventures. Still another depicts their contests of physical strength and what its exercise demands. At least twenty-five of these songs have to do with social dances; while eleven of them, as a peace loving people, have to do with wars and like struggles.

For example, let us examine one of the children's melodies, titled "Beaver's Song to Bring Rain." By way of introduction, the Beaver and the Fox-tail have gotten into difficulties and compromise seemed necessary. Hence they sang about it. Beaver said this, "So have I." Beaver sang this, and the rain came down in torrents. The melody of the song is here shown, as recorded by its author's assistants. And in commenting about this episode, its composer Frances Densmore has this to say: "This is a rhythmic, not a melodic expression, and contains only one change from its principal tone."[22]

It is this feature which often confuses the general public about genuine Indian music. Like their speech arts and oratory, native aboriginal melody is different from that developed by European peoples. To the whites, indeed, so-called native music is hum-drum, monotonous, and

84

without stimulus. It seems draggy, dead, and meaningless — primarily because its background and meaning are not understood. But its true worth must not be judged by European, in other words, by classical standards. To appreciate it, the listener must know much about the culture which produced it. This is the burden of our story. This is why this monograph is written. To know the mind and soul of the American Indian in his struggle with nature, his homelife, his worshipful attitudes, his fears, his loves, his hates, his passion for life itself, throws a flood of life on all that he does. This is what motivates our study. This is what inspires our search for his true racial image, the product of the long ages of the past.

A Modern Musician Speaks

Few there are who are competent to speak the mind of the American Indian in this field of tom-toms, indigenous rattles of simple structure, of strange flutes and sound instruments of many kinds of as strange design in their native setting to the mind of our modern music-loving world. But where such scarcity prevails, proportionate value to its attainment results. And it has been my good fortune to come under the influence of just such a specialist in my broadening acquaintanceship.

A few years ago my wife and I met such a person in a downtown hotel in crowded Los Angeles. Somewhere we had read that a Miss Elizabeth Waldo, born and reared on a vast ranch in the wild Klamath country, in the vicinity of the present Grand Coolee Dam, bordering Walla-Wallaland, was booked to explain the merits of the red man's musical instruments mentioned above. Of course our interests were aroused. We went. We listened. We were amazed at what we heard. Here is a part of it.

85

Apparently pre-Columbian America enjoyed a musical inheritance little suspected or understood by the first Europeans who came to America's shores. The best of this heritage lay to the southlands, the home of the Inca, the Maya, and kindred cultures, those surprisingly rich in their achievements and accomplishments.

For example when the Spaniards first set eyes on their temples and city structures, they were amazed at their beauty and intricate nature. So, too, with their social customs and means of entertainment. There they found flutes of rare design in common use, along with innumerable time keeping rattles and kindred devices not known in Old Spain. Moreover, the songlife of this people proved to be inspiring and ennobling.

Trained to judge in such matters in art schools in America's East, later Miss Waldo toured Latin American lands as a professional entertainer with marked success. Writing on this theme, Elizabeth Waldo says this: "In common with other countries of the Western Hemisphere, California's first music was born of Indian heritage. Unlike other areas of the Americas where the Indian music became integrated into the folklore, California Indian music remained apart — a haunting memory almost entirely lost in the mists of time. Virtually non-existent today, the Indian period can only be re-created in the imagination."[23] This craving has found expression by what has been termed the *Viva California*, the remarkable hardback publication of this name, published by Southwest Museum, Los Angeles, and art illustrated. Along with it, too, attends a PSO disk of ten Indian, Spanish, and Mexican melodies of rare charm. It is this type of product which breathes life into such interests as are ours.

The Navajo Night Chant

To omit reference to the Navajo Night Chant, now world renowned, would be to short-change the reader in regard to the red man's interest in music and songlife. Unquestionably, this Chant stands as the consummation or peak of the American Indians' achievement in the red man's musical or oral arts.

Washington Matthews, a man of rare scientific ability, was the master white mind to interpret the significance of this musical epic to the modern world. Well acquainted with the Navajo tongue and ways of life, he spent years in the study of this mystical drama on the ground in Navajoland. Hence to him we owe our thanks for its interpretation and its preservation to the interest of our modern world of music lovers.

Briefly, the Navajo Night Chant is a nine day musical performance. Both in its symbolism as well as its melody, it dates back to earliest Navajo times. Its setting is much like ancient Greek and Roman mythology, couched in tradition and preserved through the persistence of community folklore. Even in the peak of Greek philosophic thought, when interest in the creative arts with that people was running high, their populace believed in the rivalry of their gods high in the skies above Mount Olympus. Likewise with the Romans. Their traditional beginnings were on the tops of Rome's seven hills. But that was too complex. The story had to be simplified. So they invented their she-wolf and the twins, Romulus and Remus. When Remus tried to climb over his brother's wall, Romulus killed him. Thus Rome was mythically founded.

So, too, with the *Dineh* "the Navajo people," the people who do things. To these Dinehs, their Night Chant is the equivalent of Christendom's *The Messiah,* or even the ceremony of High Mass as administered by The Holy Father, Pope Paul VI at the Vatican, Rome, on Easter Sunday. Then it is that by tens of thousands the faithful gather to come under papal sacred blessing.

In fact this Navajo festivity occupies eight straight nights of intensive ceremonial action. As the centuries have advanced, this activity has grown increasingly complex, so complex in fact, that few of the Navajo priesthood today can follow its technique as built up. However, enough said on this point.

The thread of this musical drama, set to Navajo melody, takes its start with the masked mythical Grandfather of the Navajo people who yearns over his flocks in their slow painful upward climb to culture through endless centuries of time. This, the element of vicarious suffering, becomes the chief element of portrayal for hours on hours by trained priestly medicine men. When dawn breaks on the ninth day, this ceremonialism is over. Then the Dineh people give way to self-satisfaction, a purified people, and they are on their way home, the home of the simple Navajo hogan and the reaches of their boundless horizons.

In summarizing this matchless Night Chant, Washington Matthews translates its opening lines into the following English wording. Enjoy it, if you will!

His lines read this way:

1. In Tsé ghihi (meaning a mythical place)
2. In the house made of the dawn,
3. In the house made of the evening twilight,
4. In the house made of the dark cloud,
5. In the house made of the he-rain (thunder storm),
6. In the house made of the dark mist,

7. In the house made of the she-rain (light shower),

8. In the house made of pollen,

9. In the house made of the grasshoppers,

10. Where the dark mist curtains the doorway,

11. The path to which is on the rainbow,

12. Where the zigzag lightning stands high on top,

13. Where the he-rain stands on top,

14. Oh, male divinity![24]

Indian Dance Rhythm

With our first Americans, the red man's dance was as much a part of his long developed culture as were his tendencies toward hunting, his many forms of amusement, and his songlife. To try to separate one from the other is to destroy the pattern of his inward thought and to deprive him of his native heritage.

Like the ancients of the Far East, dancing came natural to those who drew breath in primeval times. Did not King David dance "before the lord with all his might" and thus gain favors divine; and did not Queen Esther gain her royal throne by dancing before her royal Lord and thereby save the lives of her people? The Scriptures give these reports as history. Why then should our pilgrim fathers, steeped in humility and religious devotion, have been so adamant about the Indian way of dancing, bedecking themselves with natural earth paint and wild bear claws, as they did?

Of course, I must say that the drumbeat as sounded on the modern dance floor is anathema to some sensitive ears. While spending long nights in intensive study at the University of Chicago, I found it so. Who could expect to study Old Testament prophets with that kind of thump-

thump going on in your very ears? But such an experience should not bias us against the steadied expert beat of the tom-tom, the loved rhythm of the red man's sensitive ear. Personally, I fully endorse Elizabeth Waldo's assertion that aboriginal American rhythm was different from the classical patterns brought from Europe. The same was true of his speech arts or oratory, his folklore, and of his dance style. And one thing more about this same matter, ever to be borne in mind when trying to understand the motive power behind his dance media. This latter, almost invariably, was couched in a devotional atmosphere and a ritualistic practice, if we will. Without clearly sensing this fundamental fact, the student often goes astray in estimating its beauty and its enduring worth.

On this same essential point it was Ernest Thompson Seton, the great American naturalist, known to almost every American youth, who said: "I have seen Russian, French, Spanish, Italian, Hungarian, Scottish, Irish, and English dances, both in their homes and in their stage presentation. And still I affirm . . . that better than any other . . . is the North American Indian." And linked to this was Seton's further statement, said he: The Indian's dancing "is clean, beautiful, dramatic, interpretive, rhythmic," and moreover it is "meritorious according to the gift of the dancer," a practice to be revered and preserved in keeping with the red man's best ways of the past.

In connection with the native aboriginal dance, almost without exception, the Indian tom-toms, together with their drummers were present. While hitherto little emphasis has been placed on training for this exercise and responsibility, the drilling was there. The good drummer was as much sought after then as now; and who would think of sponsoring the program of a modern symphonic orchestra without its drums and drummers? Who would set the rhythm's beat under such circumstances — would the flutist, the cellist, or the blower of the French horn — who would render this service?

Modern Indian Sheet Music

It is no exaggeration to say that there is an abundance of modern Indian sheet music on the market today. Much of it is a very worthy type, some of it less so, according to conditions. Should it be desired, a trusted music dealer is the answer.

The Indian compositions here cited are a part of the Carlos Troyer collection gathered many years ago, and published by the Theo. Presser Co., Philadelphia, Pennsylvania.[25] Most of these songs were gathered long before the invention of today's recording machine, hence it took time in their gathering. The first one is titled "Sunrise Call." It is a priestly melody, dedicated to the Zuñi morning god, the giver of warmth and life. This song is Zuñi's first ceremonial of the day. The sound of the song's trumpets and drums bring the village masses to the tops of their cliff dwellings to meet the spirit of the rising sun. This song is a thriller.

The next here mentioned bears title of "A Zuñian Lullaby." As might be guessed, it impersonates a Zuñi mother who disdains the rocking cradle, but wraps her baby in a baby crib, gently closes its eyes, and with low voice puts it to sleep with its own mother's singing. It, too, is an invocation to the sun god, the protector of all.

Another is called the "Indian Fire-Drill Song." It is both exciting and fascinating. Verbally, it depicts the workings of the Indian's fire drill, the instrument used for the generation of real fire, a necessity of life. Almost universally the fire stick is held to be sacred by America's red men, as it was with the ancient Egyptians.

91

A fourth song here listed is called the "Kiowa-Apache War Dance." As could be expected, it represents action to a vigorous degree. Remarkable for its rhythmical imitation of the Indians' howling whizzer, first cousin to Zuñi's bull-roarer earlier described, this instrument represents the roar of thunder and the clash of tomahawks in action. This wild chant is a mimic of Indian warfare, earlier well-known to the whites, but in this instance the deities of the attackers' hiding spot is withheld from the defenders, hence the latter are all killed. So say the Indians.

Many of these numbers, of course, were tabulated and written for vocal rendition, while others were instrumental numbers. But the sum total of them all reemphasizes the fact that their rhythm beat was typically Indian, not European, and that their purpose was reverential, in other words dedicated to their many deities. Each has its own historic setting, representing as it does, the moods, the feelings, the yearnings, the ambitions, the hopes, and the fears of those who choose to sing its abiding messages, attuned to native Indian life as it has been for ages, long before the whites came to disturb the status quo.

American Indian Decorative Arts

HAVING EXAMINED, in a very superficial way, aboriginal American Indian ways of self-entertainment, the red man's mode of gaming, his forms of religious expression, his ways of developing physical and mental dexterity, his arduous modes of getting his food supplies, together with his altruistic and friendly ways of social intermingling, and before plunging into his crash exposure to modern life let us now review his decorative arts. This search, of course, implies that these were his pre-Columbian arts, not those products from his mind and

93

hand since changed by European influence and the industrial demands of current times.

These arts naturally fall under four main heads. They are these: his pottery, his weaving, his home silver work, his shrines or sanctuary structures — these four. Let them open the way to a more appreciative attitude toward the creative ingenuity of the red man in his mastery of his native environment as it was before his simple ways met up with the more complex cultures — in the plural — which came from the East.

First of all let it be said that our American red men, even before Columbus' coming, were not adverse to self-adornment. They loved show, as we do today. Before forgotten time, they had style fever, much as we do now. The great variety of their war bonnets, the passion of their women for lipstick, hair decoration, and perfumes, to say nothing of their carved gambling sticks, offer evidence that we have not gone astray in this assumption.

Of course we do not know whether the night hawk senses the beauty of the mellowed moon light, or whether the coyote enjoys the thrill of the noonday's sun. But this we do know: The heartbeat of the American Indian throbs with delight when exposed to the glory of nature's flowers as pressed by his bare feet, and the song of the meadowlark when it sings its cheering lay.

Universally, humans respond to beauty as dry ground yearns for rain. So, in keeping with their innumerable traditions, red men crave the decorative, as do humans everywhere. Hence their pottery designs, the many mystical images which adorn their simple firesides, their homespun rugs, the spans of turquoise which dangle from their necks and about their middles, and all of the countless shrines which decorate their unspoiled landscape — these elements are self-convincing. The red man has ever loved nature's beauty, even as he cherished his own inmost thoughts.

Native Indian Pottery

When we think of Indian pottery, of course, we mean all of those implements made of nature's clay and other materials, including his vessels of woven reeds that are used for domestic purposes in the aboriginal home. This includes his cooking utensils, in part, also his water jars and bottles, even his fetishes used for devotional ends which with red men made almost without number. All of these must be combined in the term pottery, as is done elsewhere.

With today's tourist trade, such articles are gathered up as souvenirs, or reminders of where we have been. But with the scientist they may be cherished as artifacts, revealing the very nature of the red man's culture in its evolution and development.

One important factor to be remembered in this connection is that with all their flaws and imperfections, these instruments were molded by hand, not made by impersonal machinery. Again, they were *handmade*, not even shaped on the potter's wheel, as of Bible times in the Near East.

The expert eye can tell at a glance the approximate age of almost all such artifacts. In our museums and historical collections they are usually grouped according to their age and the tribal peoples by whom they were used. For example: The red men who dwelt along our Atlantic rim had one type of pottery made from local clays, while the Pueblo peoples of our Rocky Mountain elevations had quite another. So, too, with the Seminoles of the Everglades and the Eskimo of the Far North — each had its own, according to need and the materials at hand. As with their many languages, their marriage customs, their numerous ceremonials, in their pottery making each had their own forms, each their own meaningful decorations, and each their own kind of clays with which they worked, strange to say.

But, in the main, color was the line of demarcation. If unmarked and composed of plain clay, a vessel so made might mean that it was very, very old. If marked with black — that is charcoal black, or of a certain clay texture, such markings might mean the earliest trend toward ornamentation, hence ancient, indeed. In writing on this point Ruth DeEtte Simpson, field archeologist for San Bernadino County Museum, California, has this to say.

> The oldest pottery types recovered that have established the Hopi sequence (an age old type) were the black-on-white and red-and-black-on-orange wares from prior to 1300 A.D. Later strata yielded, in order, black-on-red pottery of the 14th century; Jeddito yellow wares of the 14th, 15th, and 16th centuries; Sikyatki orange and yellow pottery of the 15th, 16th, and 17th centuries; and latter "Mission" and "Early Modern" pottery. Finally, a ceramic period must be added — the Contemporary, adapted from pottery of Sikyatki style.[26]

These are the words of a specialist, trained in the science of artifact evaluation. If out to buy, don't be fooled! Go to those who know! If satisfied with the spurious, there is plenty of it with all such artifacts; but if you desire the genuine, seek it from the best markets: the hands which create the article desired, the nearest authorized Indian trading post operator, or an established institution which deals with the genuine kind of article desired.

The Indian Weaver's Art

Much which has here been said of American Indian pottery could be well repeated relative to the red man's weaving, an activity which entered into many phases of the

96

life of America's aboriginal peoples. Its development, as seen with American Indian pottery, naturally spanned many centuries of time.

Perhaps the earliest form of weaving which was used by our first Americans came with the Aleutian peoples. As we know, it is assumed that their homeland had been eastern Asia. If so, they must have been of Mongolian stock. However, so intangible is prehistoric time that credence must be given to other theories of American population origins. These might include early migrants from northern Europe by way of Greenland and otherwise. It might be, as earlier implied, that a strain of humans may have found their way from the East by way of the mythical island, Atlantis, as believed by some.

Or, prehistoric men could have come from the southern islands of the Pacific Ocean, the South Sea islands. Who knows? But this much is certain: The Americas were populated when Columbus first landed.

If the findings of the anthropologist are to be our guide, this much of the Aleutian era may be credible. Those who first forced their way to this eastern continent over that cold island-sprinkled route of sea water evidently used sea grass and perhaps the skins of sea mammals for clothing when needed. These same elements also might have been used for food as well as for clothing. If true, this means that these Aleutians knew the rudiments of the art of crude weaving. That is enough. Once such a start is made, progress usually comes with time.

A second element to challenge our red man's primitive manipulative skill was his find of native American cotton. Of course it was not of the long thread cotton now known. But there are unmistakable evidences that aboriginal Americans had native cotton. And as for animal hair of varied fineness and texture, this, too, clearly was in use as a native product in weaving.

97

A great leap from these beginning days to the present came to me in this way recently. I was asked to provide an Indian unit in connection with the first American flag to fly over the Manse of Pio Pico, the last of the Mexican governors of California. The announcement drew its thousands. As guest speaker I acquired the services of Warcaziwin, my Indian friend, of Eselata Pueblo extraction but of Sioux adoption, for the address. She appeared in native dress, cut to the nicety of a Parisian gown.

With the sombreroed native sons, sweeping the strings of their Spanish guitars with their matchless tones, as from beneath her palm covered canopy Warcaziwin stepped forth to address the throng, amazement and consternation seized the mind of those present. First, there was abject silence, then a burst of applause before she had spoken a word. The applause was not for what had been heard. It was for that which the company saw, gowned as a human being. Indeed, it must be admitted: Indian women may not always have borne the charm which Warcaziwin had that day. But some have; some have not. However, we must treat the craft of weaving, not native Indian oratory in this connection.

While America's yardage mills pour forth their products for human body coverage as well as for a thousand and one added usages today, if you know where to go, you can see a true Indian maiden at work at her spinning today, much like those of the Far East in their desert homes as of the long ago. If it be a Navajo rug, a variegated shawl, or a pony's blanket that you want, come, let us see!

There in yonder desert, near that lonely hogan, shielded by that improvised crude sunshade made of brush boughs, is a weaving frame. Shall we go? Busily engaged, with her baby close by, is a young mother totally absorbed otherwise

98

in her weaving. The product is a ground rug of matchless beauty. The materials used are the products from the backs of animals which she, herself, guarded in yonder desert.

See how, with lightning speed, she throws that curious shuttle, driven by muscle power! It carries her yarn between the strands of the rug's warp, combed and carded by her hand through night hours while others slept. And note the expression in her eye! Should her baby move, quickly she will discover the fact, despite her abstract thinking.

That gaze of hers is toward the skies. In her subtle way she works out the pattern to be embedded in the rug before her as it develops. Hers is a dedicated task, to be interpreted only in the mystical beliefs of her people. When that job is done, there will never be another exactly like it. That which motivated this kind of work is much like the winds which blow. You may know the direction from which they come, but you cannot tell why they come nor whither they go, according to Indian mythology.

And one thing more, this worker will see to it that this rug is not without its planned imperfection. Should she perfectly close each strand of its woof, held taut by the weight of her own body, her clan spirits might thus be imprisoned in the product before her and be angered with confinement, hence bring mischief to her own life and to those of her household. All of these principles, and much more, are involved in a genuine Indian weaving art.

Again, should you be satisfied with the spurious, you can find what pass as Indian rugs anywhere. But should you desire the genuine, call at the lonely hogan in the desert; you'll receive a warm welcome, I can assure. Or trek to the nearest licensed Indian trading post; but be prepared for prices not comparable to those quoted for products put together by machine power, and checked at every turn of their development by electrically controlled gadgets. Indeed, the Indian way is slow; but its products are genuine.

The Turquoise Craft

We have looked into the eyes of the dedicated Navajo mother rug weaver. In our unobserved position we caught a glimpse of the awe with which she spun her yarns and wove her mysterious figures into the warp and woof of her sacred rugs, the carriers of her deities. Earlier we caught a glimpse of Chief Seattle's vision of his Dwamish peoples, and how their multiplied spirits swarmed over the hills and dales of their ancient homeland when the electric lights of the city of Seattle were to come on.

And again, go with me to Cologne, southwest Germany, where Cologne Cathedral still stands. It is the finished product of medieval artistry in stone, the consummation of Renaissance church construction of the Middle Ages. The stone walls above its doorways are thronged with marvelous stone saints placed there centuries ago by the best craftsmen of their time. Its flying buttresses, its towers reaching toward the skies, even its fire walls at the edge of its roof tops are decorated with similar effigies of meaningful figures in stone, reminders of what Europeans constructed before America was known to Christopher Columbus. A later poet was moved to pen these lines as to why Cologne's uniqueness for that day's chiseled artistry, viz.:

> "In the elder days of art, workmen toiled with
> ceaseless care;
> Each minute and unseen part — for the gods see
> everywhere."

100

So it was with Europeans; and so it was with the red men of America. Each carries its own fetishes. Each is awed by the mysteries of the heavens above and the wonders of the earth beneath our feet. Hence our inquiry as to the why of the string of turquoise beads strung around the necks of both men and women of this high country, so-called Puebloland, and the strange nuggets of this greenish stone, imbedded in silver, lashed about the middles of these up-country native red men.

One modest question presses for an answer. How came the name turquoise? Historians tell us that it is a Turkish term borrowed from what today is our Near East. What it was called by America's aboriginals I do not know. But it seems that the Mohaves of prehistoric California mined this greenish stone in their mountains. Somehow it found its way to Turkish lands, the land of the Mohammedans, who gave it its name. Small world, isn't it! But to say the least, among the Pueblo and the Navajo peoples, its turquoise artists dwell today.

A spokesman for this high mountain people says this as to the sanctity of this body ornament: "If the turquoise has been pulverized, dyed, molded — who cares? These will never take the place in real esthetic value of the simple and heavy ornaments made many decades ago in primitive style by the Navajos (and others) in their own hogans for their own adornment. And this is true. Every attitude of these high mountain peoples, whether for ceremonial purpose or for fun, vindicates the rightness of this evaluation. But let us see their artisans at work. Then, perhaps, we will understand why their devotion to this attractive greenish stone, abundant and colorful though it may be embraced in its white silver framework.

It is to be assumed that the same principle of development from the simple to the complex has been maintained in the Indian turquoise crafts which we have seen in their mastery of pottery and weaving skills. And the countless artifacts to this end, now safely housed under roof in our museums and collegiate halls vindicate the truth of this assumption.

But how do these artisans go about their tasks; from whence do their materials come; what tools do they possess for their work; how do they acquire the required training for their aptitudes; what motivates them for such detailed tasks; when finished, where are the markets for their products? These and many other related questions crowd upon us. But limited space confines our response. To the specialists we must go for information.

In a word, the tools with which these red men now work and have long labored in the development of their unique crafts, of many kinds, might well have been found in the workshops of the medieval artisan, "the butcher, the baker, the candlestick maker."

First of all, even today, these products, almost to a unit, are strictly homemade goods, and handmade, too. The tools used, likewise, are very simple. Once, undoubtedly, for hammers they used chipped stone, for melting pots they used clay bowls, with hot charcoal for heat. Yes, for untold ages they also knew the up and down drill, propelled by the leather thong pinned to its upright stem. Also for plungers, as nails, they resorted to nature's hard, sharp animal teeth. Even today, all that is required at their skilled hands is a mold, a hammer, a small screwdriver, a pair of tweezers, a small section of a railroad iron, and his workmen are ready to go.

Having silently stood by these skilled artisans while they worked, I have been amazed at their skill in bringing forth the shapliest reproduction of the yucca's bloom or the wings of the honey bee seeking its nectar. This being the case, is it any wonder that they ply their trade with reverence toward their creator, the giver of all, the soul of nature? Search where you may throughout the earth, for simplicity of mind, patience of effort, and consummate enjoyment of the finished product. I know of nothing to be compared to the intrinsic value of these red men's products, not even the work of the fine diamond smiths of Brussels, Belgium, the renowned home of those who buy today's jewelry.

American Indian
Sacred Shrines

W E HAVE ALL HEARD of the Seven Wonders of the
World. These were among them, if my memory
does not trick me: the pyramids of Egypt, the
Colossus of Rhodes, and the Hanging Gardens of Babylon.

Egypt's Great Pyramid, but a few miles south from
Cairo, occupies almost thirteen acres of land. Moreover, its
top towers more than 470 feet toward Egypt skies. In turn
the noted Hanging Gardens, built by King Nebuchadnezzer
for his charming Median Queen who yearned for her
mountain home, then amidst Babylon's desert wastes, com-

prised a totally artificial set of show gardens, spaced here and there with trees and flowers, resting on shaky pillars of dried brick common to that day's construction. Now, like many another wonder of ancient times, it is rubble.

But what about China's Great Wall, or the Leaning Tower of Pisa, Italy, or Britain's Stonehenge — are not these wonders or shrines of bygone days? So the question arises: what is a *wonder*, what is a *shrine?* To answer this question before we go farther, let us consult a handy word book, a good dictionary.

My word book tells me that a shrine is a spot held sacred, such as a burial ground intended for the covering of old bones or unused artifacts. But are we interested in *old bones*, as such, unless they bore evidence of having had eminence in the past? So, let us look farther!

Another definition of shrines is this: It may be the tomb of a saint; a hallowed object, such as a sacred altar; a thing or place consecrated to a deity; or even a jewel, enshrined in velvet. But to a specialist who deals in words, a shrine such as the Mosque of Omar; the Taj Mahal of India; St. Peter's, Rome; or Canterbury Cathedral, England; it must have worshipful significance. It must be a thing or place which carries men's minds heavenward or godward. It must have worshipful meaning. This is a shrine. In other words, a shrine is a holy place.

Shrines of America's Mound Builders

As for American Indian shrines, they are almost numberless. They are to be found everywhere. For example: Let us go back to America's mound builder days, clearly prehistoric times.

Who were these mound builders? From whence came they? Why did they build their many mounds from the mouth of the Mississippi River to its source, then eastward

106

up the Ohio River from end to end? This is a problem for archeologists to answer.

One of these structures whose earth walls are miles in length is known as Old Fort Ancient. It borders on the rough banks of the Little Miami River which flows nearly three hundred feet below. As a boy I tramped over its broad acres, reliving ages gone by. Long before there were modern bulldozers to lift tons of earth at a single jab, these walls were piled up by handmade thread baskets by human muscle power. Its walls which rise from five to twenty feet in height have been built as a safeguard against other marauding primitive enemies of that ancient time.

The Old Fort, itself, covers many acres of ground. On its western fringe, a level, open area prevails. It is thought that in ancient times it served as a corral or closed space for the capture of roving buffalo which occasionally came that way. And at the center of its enclosure, closed-in mounds of added height still challenge the public; perchance these served as a protection to the main sanctuary or altar on which sacrifices were offered to the deities worshipped. Hence it served as a meeting spot for the elite, but as a *shrine* in the best sense of this word.

About fifty miles northeast from Old Fort Ancient lies a second major mound of mound builder origin of singular size and importance. It is located in Adams County, Ohio, and is known as Serpent Mound. Some archeologists hold that both Old Fort Ancient as well as Serpent Mound are as ancient in years as are the pyramids of Egypt and China's Great Wall. Others have divided the age of these mound builders into three separate periods: those of the Hopewell era, the Adena, and the Fort Ancient era. Powerful groups of primitive cultures moved across the American continent north and south, east and west during these eras, each leaving its trail of conquest behind

107

it in its own barbarous fashion, along with its peculiar artifacts.

Serpent Mound is one of the most remarkable remains of this long mound builder period. The Serpent itself is of cobra fashion, with flattened head and neck. From its head to the tip of its coiled tail it is stretched over some thirteen hundred and thirty feet in length, its body following the curved contour of a small stream which still flows close below.

The curved mounds of this earth serpent range from three to eight feet above the surrounding landscape according to location; and in width they range from three to fifteen feet in breadth. At the serpent's head is a curious mound whose use, as yet, has not been unraveled. It, too, is roundish in shape, thought by some to represent an egg or a frog, in the act of being swallowed by the snake. For guessing purposes this slight mound helps to enliven the mythology of those ancient times.

That this mound was a shrine has been almost assured. Its location as well as its design rightly suggest this. When we think of the sacred position which the snake held with the native red men of America, the very size and form of this vast serpentine mound leaves little question as to its purpose as a worship center, a sacred spot of its peoples, the mound builders of the long ago. It must have been a shrine to which countless numbers of our pre-Columbian red men came from near and far to pay their devotions, as have humans for ages past, everywhere, expressing their inmost devotion to their deities.

Whatever this silent Serpent Mound may have been, let us repeat, it bears all of the ear marks of sanctity to those who put it there. To them it must have been their St. Peter's, their Canterbury Cathedral, their Westminster Abbey, London. But before closing this brief description of America's mound builder era, let us catch a glimpse at recent finds of these same mysterious people as disclosed

108

by the archeologist's spade at the Old Cahokia Mound, one of the largest of them all, near the mouth of the Ohio River, where it joins the father of America's inland waters, the Mississippi.

The Archeologist's
Spade Still Digs

A MERICA'S SHRINE BEDS offer the trained archeol-
ologist a wealth of finds for an indefinite future. It
is with the untrained that public concern rests. All
should be aware that in the search for artifacts, inexperi-
enced curiosity can be costly. And more: We should be
reminded that to our first Americans their shrines and
burying grounds were sacred; hence the most painstaking
care should be used in the exhuming or the exploration
of all such sacred sites.

Be this as it may, recently a revealing era of prehistoric

111

American life of the mound builder period has been exposed near Eldred, Illinois, the seat of America's ancient Cahokia Mound. In size it is one of the largest mounds of all left behind by that ancient culture. In digging into its depths three levels of ancient village life have been laid bare. Its earliest dates back to 3000 B.C., it is said, the age of the Egyptian pyramids. At its upper strata it carried life of approximately the 1200 A.D. era, or three hundred years before the coming of Columbus.[27]

And what did the diggers find? This is a pertinent question. They found that these Easterners bore many of the traits of their ancient ancestors who came from Asia by way of the Bering Strait. They also assumed that their immediate forebears were the fathers of certain of our western Indian tribes, which is not surprising.

The abundance of the spearheads unearthed was, indeed, revealing. Also fragments of animal bones, long extinct, as well as bits of used iron likewise were found. The harvest was rich in such artifacts, to be distributed to the leading universities and museums throughout America for safekeeping for the enlightenment of generations yet unborn.

California's Fifty-Seven Shrines

NOW TO OUR PACIFIC RIM in our quest, far removed from our red men's shrines of America's prairies and the times of the ancient mound builders. Before closing this brief sketch of American Indian shrines, by invitation, let us trek with an intimate friend as guide to California's venerable "Fifty-Seven Shrines," the original home of one of this Golden State's ancient native peoples, residents of its dry deserts, centuries before its discovery of gold at Sutter's Mill. A trusty guide, long a resident in this bleak area, will lead the way.

Our guide is Paul Wilhelm, by name. His home is at

Thousand Palms Oasis, a curious landmark. His many palm trees, enlivened by its strange lake of crystal waters close by, are most inviting on a hot summer's day. Both form the heart of these surrounding desert wilds. Above his head towers the snows of San Gorgonia's Peak, fourteen thousand feet above the nearby Pacific Ocean. About this I know, for alone, I crested its height and found the surveyor's marker to that effect.

Personally friendly, he is fortunate in two ways. His palm trees, like those of Africa's desert sands, yield their luscious fruit for many months. And more, those same life-giving waters, the results of underground rivers, fed by melted snows, are forced to the surface by the stubborn San Andres' troublesome fault which stretches from San Francisco to the Mexican border and beyond.

First our path lies along an Indian trail, ages old. It was worn there by Indian maidens' feet carrying water in their ollas toward the heights of Bee Rock Mesa above. But stop! What is that small circle of stones, with a larger one in its center, at your feet! Is not it a shrine, or was it merely a gossip point where brown-eyed maidens exchanged reports of young braves' glances atop yonder mesa the day before? Who knows? Anyway, this is not the Fifty-Seven Shrines Trail. It lies farther on.

As described by Paul, our guide, the trail over which we were to pick our way was "bone-dry, with scant vegetation." Creosote bushes, grotesquely stunted, their leaves folded desperately inward to retain every bit of moisture acquired, marked our pathway. Within plain view to the west rose "the two-mile-high blue summit of San Jacinto Mountain," another high shrine of this vast desert region. This whole charmed isolated region lay in perpetual quietude, a little world of its own.

Finally, we stand at the southern border of Bee Rock Mesa, a Gibraltar of this wild desert country.

114

Again, stop! Look! What is that heap of stones, of every size, at our feet? Paul steps forth to tell us. Under this same blazing summer's sun, three years before, he first discovered this trail. He says that behind his Indian guide, Pablo Arroz, he struggled up these same sharp switch-backs of big Bee Rock Mesa to this very point. Nearing this summit Arroz turned aside. He sought quietude. He picked up a stone, placed it on this mound of rocks; then moved along the trail.

And why this act? This was the Indians' way of approach to their revered shrines. But almost two miles of such stone piles lay ahead, each with its own forgotten story. To be sure of their number, on his return from this trail's "Holy of Holies," its terminus, ringed with red stones, he returned to count one by one these sacred mementos of the past, to be sure of their number. Yes, there were fifty-seven in all, the lonely trail well marked between them.

Today, not a living soul dwells on Bee Rock Mesa. Like Chief Seattle's people, the Dwamish, their originals are all gone. Floods of whites of every description have moved in. Palm Springs, California, with its host of merry-makers, is but thirty miles or so away. Indio, California, another of our windswept tourist stopping points, lies nestled in this same palm-strewn desert country. As the shades of unmarked time settle on these hallowed high-lands of Bee Rock Mesa, of Phantom Hills, of the clay butte known as Squaw Hill, Cragg Bluff, Elephant Butte, and Gaunt Ridge, this country's main high points, if we had spirit eyes to see and spirit ears to hear, might we not be sensitive to the imagined laughs, the shouts, the songs of those red primitives who, ages ago, cherished these wild desert lands?

It is out of this kind of mythical thinking, this kind

115

of ranging over the red man's travel-trails of the past, that the love of traditional history of America's long past is reborn. Let it be kindled in the hearts of all, at its best; for the love of nature's ways is the red man's heritage to be conveyed to America's cosmic generations yet unborn. This is our message. This is our story of the Trail of Fifty-Seven Shrines, on the shores of the Pacific rim, within the golden state of California.

What of America's Future?

AMERICA'S PAST is known to us all. It amounts to about this: prehistoric time and historic time. Measured in terms of centuries, its aboriginal or beginning span must have been much longer than that of the over-flooding by Europeans and their descendants. Today the United States alone boasts of a composite population of more than 200,000,000 people, come from all parts of our earth. Of this number the progeny or offspring of its first sons may have been small, even at their peak of power. Today they comprise but a small minority now

117

engaged in the mastery of the North American continent.

Already nine American astronauts have circumnavigated the moon and planted the Stars and Stripes there, 250,000 miles from America's shores. The products of our mines and mills are to be found in every corner of our earth. The language spoken here is understood everywhere. The heart-passion of the world's billions look to our great land for protection and guidance. America's free school system stands as the model to be followed by all mankind. In cumulative wealth and might, collective America has no rival. But what of this native minority within its boundaries? What is its destiny? Is it to be swallowed up and forgotten as time moves on? Actually, is the American Indian a vanishing people, a decadent group, an ineffective race of people within America's borders? Let us see.

America's Destiny Lies Ahead

In previous pages strong emphasis has been laid on the imaginative powers of our first Americans. This needed trait seems to be inherited in the cumulative culture of the red man. Their young dream their way into adult attitudes as naturally as flowers bloom. In nature's forces they see much of the spirit world, finding little difference between the imagined and the real. This is a primary feature in their physical and mental makeup, as we have seen. It stands out prominently in all that they do and say.

In much of life are we not prone to indulge those of tender years in their imaginative dreaming? Perhaps this is because in later years, experience has taught us that all is not gold that glitters, and realities are not what in youth-years they seem to be. While hoping for the best, by axiom we know, along with the flower, "into each life some rain must fall." These are experiences known to all. But still, even in scientific research and exploration, we stand prone to dreaming our way into the unknown so that the desired may become a reality. Again, by inherent nature, this is one of the gifts which our primitive Americans, by inheritance, are in a position to bequeath to our scientific age.

In his perilous trek toward free Canada, with his food supplies gone, his women and children freezing, his choice brave, Chief Looking Glass, dead at his feet, and surrounded by three mounted white armies, it was Chief Joseph (Nez Perce) who said this: "It is the young men who say yes or no," when it comes to fighting battles. Stripped of his resources, Chief Joseph then declared, "I will fight no more forever." So it is with American Indian youth today. They no longer fight with bow and arrow as they once did. But to make headway in modern complex society, they are forever faced with the demands of specialization so much a part of modern life. This challenge we are to explore.

My wife, at age sixteen, was valedictorian of her high school class. Her science teacher, a visionary fellow, urged that in her parting words at graduation she picture ships of passage in the skies as a future achievement. She hesitated. But she complied. You know what happened. Laughs came from every quarter. That was decades ago. Today, not so. At certain times now, loaded airplanes carrying scores of people and tons of merchandise from every part of the world, whisk above our dwelling. She has spanned these years. Times have changed. The rush of progress has been intense. This today is our modern world. He who would reap its rewards must qualify according to its demands. America now has entered its Space Age, with no space limitations to its destiny.

Modern American Indian Life

A QUARTER OF A CENTURY ago this heart wail was wrenched from the lips of a young Indian freshly home from military service in Europe. In anguish of soul he said this as he returned to reservation life.

> The tragedy is no less pitiable because without hateful intent. Neither government nor citizens have proposed it. It is simply the narrative of a nature race thrust aside by a mighty civilization. . . .
> No wonder that we are not the strong . . . people who entered these reservations a half century ago. No

wonder the "music of life" has gone out! No wonder we are heartbroken and disconsolate! No wonder that under the "doom of perpetual childhood" we "croon about our dead past."

If recorded, this same moan of despondency could be heard today from many red men's lips who dwell on and off of our numerous government reservations that are controlled by our federal government's Bureau of Indian Affairs.

But how valid, how just is such a wail? Before rendering judgment on this point, let us review what has been done to date for this dependent minority of the American population over the past century. Perhaps such a review may indicate where America should go from here in this important matter.

The fact reminds us that federal law now is sovereign in all parts of the United States. This simply means that all citizens and dwellers within our national borders are subject to this law so long as they make America their home. It further means that those individual and collective rights, guaranteed in our federal Constitution, today are the rights of all.

As for the Indian reservation system, it was our government's way of throwing the blanket of protection about the interests of the many tribes of red men who dwelt within our expanding national boundaries. On these reservations today, nearly all of which lie beyond the Mississippi River, dwell approximately one-half of our native Indian people, governed by tribal, state, and federal processes, determined by conditions established.

However, the demands of modern life have brought sweeping changes to many such Indian individuals and families. The earning of a living is one of these. It is life's main essential. And to meet this requirement, job training

122

and job placement are prime necessities. In other words, modern educational experience is an essential, along with the know-how suited to the hour.

Indian Schools and Colleges

From our earliest colonial day to the present, schooling at the schoolhouse has been an obsession with the American people. It was true of the town meeting school of New England; it was true of the one-room schoolhouse of our growing West; and it is true today of continental United States from coast to coast. For its leadership America banks on its schools.

For the first three centuries of our national life, schooling for Indians was the work of the missionaries. As early as 1568, for example, the Jesuit Fathers organized a school for Indian children from Florida. Later the Franciscan order did likewise, as also did numerous of the Protestant sects which took an interest in the American Indians. After our American Congress was set up this same urge expressed itself. Hence by 1842 there were thirty-seven such schools for Indian children operated by the American government; and by 1881 this number had increased to 106, we are told.

But by 1964 there were 263 such institutions for instruction for Indian children and youths, including those of elementary and secondary schools, within our national borders operated under our Bureau of Indian Affairs, along with its many other major concerns to be administered by this the oldest instrument of our federal government. Hence, almost from its beginning, Indian education, too, as with secular education, the schoolroom for Indians, has been of deep concern for red men's growing children, amidst the complexities of current life.

When bells rang for the school year 1964, there were

132,654 American Indian children, ages from 6 to 18 years of age, registered in our federal government schools. Because of state movements in our West, almost 10 percent of this number were dropped from these federal schools, since the states of California, Idaho, Michigan, Texas, Washington, and Wisconsin provided their own public instruction for its Indian children at state expense, if desired. Even at this rate it is said fully one-third of all children from Indian homes, whatever the road conditions or weather might be, were trained by these federal government agencies.[29]

Of course the center of this system was Haskell Institute, located in the heart of the nation, at Lawrence, Kansas. Its facilities for applied and academic work for Indian youth were almost ideal. Today it is rated as a high school and junior college, approved by the Association of Schools and Colleges of that part of the United States. Its campus included approximately 1,200 acres of the best land in that part of our great West, and its usable buildings number around 100 or more. Its student body of recent years has served some 88 tribal groups, well known to our great country; and its courses of study, in the main, train for occupational and professional careers.

Indian Scholarships and Aid Funds

These days it has become almost axiomatic that for every educational need, aid funds are present. A short time ago my doorbell rang. I answered. There stood a man of sixty, straight as an arrow's shaft. He handed me an improvised drawing of his name. It was this _M_ , meaning Two Mountains. He was a Seneca. In broken English he said, "Me no steal. Want work." His face was clean. His clothes worn. His toes shown through. I met his need. He left refreshed. He was every inch an Indian.

124

Soon afterward I read this challenge in one of America's widely used newssheets "Navajos are a proud people. They ask for no handouts." They announce "a 10-Million Dollar College Scholarship Fund" for those who can qualify. This was the act of their supreme council, held at headquarters, Window Rock, Arizona. So it goes today, almost every educational institute of collegiate standing holds hands forth to students of all color lines who can qualify.

A century ago the Navajo nation was in deep distress. They strove to block the way to California's coveted goldfields. In revolt, a century ago, they had to deal with Kit Carson, the champion of our western frontier. Their entire nation, 20,000 in number, were marched off to prison at the point of America's guns. Then followed their treaty at old Fort Sumner in New Mexico. Since then they have become, by ceaseless labor and economies, 100,000 strong, the largest Indian tribe in numbers in all America. In brief, this is why they stand as the model of modern Indian education.

Through dint of suffering and tears, their sparse dry acres of a hundred years ago have now grown to the grand total of more than twenty-three million acres, rich in mineral resources, iron, coal, uranium, and kindred supplies. Moreover its underlying rocks appear surcharged with oil and like materials well suited to America's industrial growth for tomorrow. Moreover, their high mountain climate, though rugged, seems well suited to America's recreational demands, hence they are readied for whatever is to be.[30]

One of their moves, recently announced, is the Navajo university already in the making. Its enrollment is designed for any Navajo who is eighteen years of age or over, whatever his educational preparation may have been. Courses in mathematics, tool making, cattle raising, farm-

125

ing, engineering, business administration, and on and on, are now in their molding stage. Backed by almost unlimited financial power, this movement gives promise of becoming an infinite educational blessing for countless centuries to come for the cultural interests of our great Southwest. This, with standards set by our professional schools and colleges of America, is cutting new trails for Indian education for America's unbounded future.[31]

Government Policy Broadened

Historically, policies or principles of government develop slowly. The Magna Carta, the foundation stone of British liberties, presents a fitting example. Signed on the plain of Runnymede, June 15, 1215, in clear view of the British king's present royal palace named Windsor Castle, near London, the realm's barons established their constitutional rights against the arbitrary will of their monarch.

By the Treaty of Paris five and a half centuries later, 1783, the independence of Britain's thirteen American colonies was recognized, after which six years later the Constitution of the United States was born. It was the product of a hundred and fifty years of tested colonial experience on our side of the Atlantic Ocean.

Here Indo-American relations were vital. Their basis lay in land controls, in the ill-defined boundaries of forest and fen, and in the good things of primitive American life. As these relations grew, policies of government developed. Internal and external safety and peace were rights of all and had to be protected. Hence an armed force was sustained, termed the War Department, to see that these prerequisites prevailed. To its Bureau of Indian Affairs all matters affecting Indian interests had their origin. Under these primitive conditions this bureau had an early beginning.

126

Since then, however, great have been the changes through which America has passed. Our national territories have expanded from coast to coast. Today our national interests are worldwide. To keep pace with existing conditions, a modernization of the working machinery of our Bureau of Indian affairs seemed vital. At present its functions are administered by two departments of our federal government, the Department of Interior and the Department of Health, Education, and Welfare, as we have seen. However, as governmental administration has become increasingly complex in keeping with all branches of current public life, Indo-American interests cried aloud for an upgrading of its system of administration. This cry found voice, July 8, 1970, in President Nixon's joint address to Congress of that date. In brief, these are its contents.

The President first cited the fact that our native Indians are "the most deprived and most isolated minority group in our nation." Continuing, he declared, "On virtually every scale of measurement . . . the condition of our Indian people stands at the bottom." "One of the saddest aspects of Indian life in the United States," he asserted, "is the low quality of Indian education." Dropouts from school, said he, "are twice our national average," and under federal supervision "is less than six school years" per enrolled child.

The President further urged that "the health of the Indian people still lags 20 to 25 years behind that of the general population." Moreover, he cited the fact that the "average age of death among Indians is 44 years, about one-third less than the national average." But the page glared when the words were read that "infant mortality is nearly 50 percent higher for Indians," than that for our general population. These conditions, he insisted, were not right and should not be allowed to continue in a land proud of its health record.

As for the government's federal policy of administration, the President urged the adoption by the Congress of new corrective measures for the administration of Indian affairs under the following nine heads as guidelines.

1. The specific rejection by Congress of the Termination Principle. The President urged that the basis of any new national policy must be the strengthening of the Indian's sense of autonomy without threatening his sense of community. Under this principle we must assure the Indian that he can assume control of his own life without being separated involuntarily from the tribal group.
2. The right to Control and Operate Federal Programs should be encouraged, said the President. This included close cooperation with the Federation of Economic Opportunity both on and off of Indian reservations for the economic welfare of our Indian citizenry.
3. Restoration of "Sacred Lands" revered by the Indians, such as the Blue Lake Shrine of the Taos Indians of New Mexico and others
4. Indian Education, suited to the demands of modern life
5. Economic Development of natural resources, including federal loan grants, Indian-administered under federal supervision
6. Increased federal appropriations for meeting Indian domestic needs
7. Special attention to Indian urban needs: In this connection it was urged that as with our general population, the drift of our Indian population is toward our major cities for employment purposes. Nearly half of our Indo-Americans today dwell in our urban centers.
8. Modernized Indian Guardianship over trustee funds likewise was urged. This need runs into many lines, including mineral rights and scenic

developments of many kinds.

9. Elevation of the Commissioner of Indian Affairs to the position of Assistant Secretary of Indian and Territorial Affairs: While racewise the Indian today comprises our smallest colorline minority, culturally he comprises our richest aboriginal heritage, as is known to all. So profoundly has he affected the course of our national development that his welfare has become of supreme importance to the American nation.[32]

On July 8, 1970, these were the concern of the President of the United States as he pled the case of our Amerindians before our national Congress. Based on his rich experiences in public life, his sincerity of appeal came with convincing power. What the results are to be, of course, lies with America's tomorrow. He has spoken. Others must lead the way.

Indians Who Lead
the Way

THOSE OF INDIAN EXTRACTION who today lead the way to America's tomorrow clearly are as gifted in character and abiding zeal as were their racial spokesmen of bygone days. For example: When the Council of Greenville met in the old Northwest Territory in 1795, east of the Mississippi, there was no dearth of Indian statescraft. Their spokesmen then were such chiefs as Tecumseh, Cornplanter, Farmer's Brother, Little Turtle, and many others. The tribal groups then concerned were the Wyandots, Delawares, Shawnees, Ottowas, Chippewas,

131

Miamis, Kickapoos, and thousands more who were deeply concerned in the outcome of those crucial days.

Now the names of Indian leaders who grace the pages of current public affairs are like the stars of heaven for number. To enumerate all in this brief undertaking, of course, would be far from our aim and purpose. But to tip the hat, or should we say the hand in Indian fashion, in recognition to a few of those who today carry large responsibility in civic matters and needed social reform, clearly is within our province. This is a part of our passion for our times. This is well within our purpose at hand.

Louis R. Bruce — Commissioner of Indian Affairs

Like many of our leading American Indians, Louis R. Bruce is a self-made, modern, career-minded citizen. He was born on the Onondaga Reservation near Syracuse, New York, and raised on the St. Regis Reservation in Northern New York. His father was a Mohawk and his mother an Ogalala Sioux, of which he is rightly proud. As a young man, Bruce attended Syracuse University, the hunting grounds of his paternal forebears. There, much to his lasting satisfaction, he won honors in scholarship as well as pole vaulting.

Imbued with a passion for public service, Mr. Bruce has used his talents in many fields, one of which is animal husbandry. Today, he owns and operates a 600-acre dairy farm in Richfield Springs, New York, stocked with the best milk yielding animals known to that part of America's East. For nine years, he served on the Board of Directors of the Dairymen's League Cooperative, known world-wide for its progressive policies. He was Youth Education and Public Relations Director for that organization. Along with his farm interests, Mr. Bruce assisted in the supervision of a

132

farm youth program, similar to the 4-H Clubs of America, its members benefiting by his masterful skills and management.

Bruce also became deeply involved in social and ethnic matters. For years he was national chairman of the National Boy Scouts of America, a member of America's National Council of Churches and served as executive director of the National Congress of American Indians.

It was this gifted man whom President Nixon selected as head of the United States Bureau of Indian Affairs in August, 1969.

Under Commissioner Bruce's competent leadership, vital changes have been introduced into the operations of the Bureau in keeping with the President's announced new Indian policy. First, the trust principle as applied to Indian lands is to be strictly enforced. Technical aids for the employment of Indians in suitable occupations are to be offered. Government underwriting of financial assistance is to be emphasized, and fourth, active help "in the co-ordination of state, local and private resources" for the uplift of our American Indians is to be encouraged.

These four points, together with the policy of training Indians to manage their own affairs in modern life now stands as the bases of Commissioner Bruce's policy for the Bureau of Indian Affairs.

Surely, with such leadership, a new day is dawning for our First Americans.[33]

Chief W. W. Keeler — a Modern Industrialist

Mr. W. W. Keeler, Head Chief of the Oklahoma Cherokee Nation, today stands as a model of our merged aboriginal and European American cultures. Born in Texas, April 5, 1908, he has risen from the ranks to his present position of leadership in our cosmopolitan American

133

society. At this writing, he is chairman of the board of directors of our National Association of Manufacturers as well as chief officer of the far flung Phillips Petroleum Company as well as the Independent National Gas Company, with headquarters in his home city, Bartelsville, Oklahoma.

Mr. Keeler is in possession of a keen business mind, aptly fitted to modern needs. Over the years, moreover, he has shown himself deeply interested in the changing current demands of modern American life. First, he finished high school in his home town, Bartelsville. Then he spent three years at Kansas University, Lawrence, Kansas, in undergraduate study. He then transferred to the College of the Ozarks, Clarksville, Arkansas, from which he received the honorary degree, LLD, for his achievements. Not satisfied, he then went for special engineering study at the Colorado College of Mines, well known for the thoroughness of its work, from which he was awarded the honorary degree of Doctor of Engineering.

Then followed academic honors thick and fast. First his Alma Mater, the University of Kansas awarded to him its Distinguished Alumni Service Citation, the highest honor granted by that Institution. In 1966 he was elected to the State of Oklahoma's Hall of Fame. In 1969 by The University of Oklahoma he was showered by its highest honor, its Distinguished Service Citation, from which quickly followed the Golden Plate Award and his induction into the American Academy of Achievement, named a "Significant Sig," a member of its famed Sigma Chi fraternity. Hence, academically, he stood a Civitan International by 1970, the date of this writing.

But Keeler proved to be more than a scholar. He is humanitarian in action as well. He is a Mason of the coveted 33rd. degree also. In its body he is a member of

134

its Legion of Honor. And through it he was devoted to the work of its Order of DeMolay, by which he was awarded the emblem of Silver Beaver; and with similar honors by the Boy Scouts of America.

As to Keeler's civic activities, these too were national as well as world wide. In the year 1961 he was named as head of a group of experts for the refurbishing of the work of our national Bureau of Indian Affairs. The year before this, 1960, he had been sent by Washington D.C. as head of our first U.S. Petroleum Industry Exchange Commission to study the oil industry in Russia. Since then he has given much of time and energies to the work of our National Petroleum Council.

It is this Amerindian of affairs who penned these lines of counsel for America's youth of tomorrow — Indian and non-Indian alike. They come freighted with tested wisdom. Said he:

> Today's young people, unlike their grandparents or parents, have been born into a world of rapid and tumultuous change. They are committing their talents and energy to cope with the challenges of this changing world.
>
> Indeed, if history were likened to a river, our young people could be considered the bold adventurers challenging the "white water" of change, while their elders float cautiously along the bank seeking still waters. The daring spirit of today's young generation can only be admired. Yet, in their enthusiasm to ride the rapids of change, can these bold adventurers foresee the sunken rocks and hidden eddies that lie ahead? Do these young pioneers possess the backlog of experience that will enable them to recognize the subtle signs of danger?
>
> A respect for experience and a sense of history have always been dominant forces in the life of the American Indian. And perhaps this is the reason for

135

his enduring vitality despite oppression and abuse.

The young generation of today must recognize that history is a great teacher. It must be questioned, it must be pierced with an analytical eye, but it can never be dismissed.

I have faith young people will listen to the lessons of the past, and that motivated by their idealistic enthusiasm, they will overcome the challenges of the future.

So wrote Mr. Keeler, Chief of the Oklahoma Cherokee Nation to those who would read. His counsel is ours now, so long as printed time endures.

Bradley Blue — Heads U.S. Court of Claims

One of America's most tangled judicial relationships is the work of its Indian Court of Claims. For decades at the beginning of American jurisprudence, as is well known, the American Indian was looked upon as beyond the pale of the law. He had no rights, other than those prescribed in the many treaties entered into by our national government. He could not sue or be sued for damages sustained, other than by the processes laid down in the treaties to which we have just referred which were almost numberless and indefinite in kind.

However, that status was changed by act of Congress in 1946 which gave the right of economic citizenship under the law. Today Bradley Blue, a Lumbee tribesman, a resident of North Carolina, sits at the head of this court, with headquarters in Washington D.C.

Mr. Blue studied law at the Cumberland University School of Law, Williamsburg, Kentucky, where he demonstrated his active mind. On graduation, he moved to Kingsport, Tennessee, where he quickly established himself in his profession as city judge. Then he was elected as president of his local Bar Association, and then as advocate of the State American Legion.

Surrounding him in boyhood, color-lines in his world were drawn closely. There were three: White, Black, Red — a type of segregation which to him was exceedingly repulsive. Blue studied law to bring about a change. Today he leads America's Indian Court of Claims, called to that post by President Nixon.

Judge Blue is quoted as saying that in establishing justice, "one of the most difficult and time-consuming tasks is to weigh the opinions of various experts on acreage boundary lines and land usage at the time the transaction took place," perhaps a century or so before. Those who frequent our courts today, of course, are familiar with this complexity. Many of Judge Blue's decrees run into many millions of dollars in favor of his fellow countrymen, the Amerindians, but justice must be done. Only right must prevail in the law courts of America's "Today and Tomorrow."[35]

Raymond Nakai — His Administrative Career

Raymond Nakai, at heart a Navajo of the Navajos, is at present chairman of the great Navajo Tribal Council whose headquarters are at Window Rock, Arizona, near Gallup, New Mexico. His is a leading voice for all things Indian in our vast Southwest today.

Raymond Nakai was born in the wide open Lukuchuka country, but a few miles from the memorable Canyon De Chelle, cliff dweller's homes of the long, long ago. Even his present home at Window Rock is but a short distance from this vast natural shrine through whose gigantic glassless window extends a view of the boundless view of desert wastes in all directions. Like many another

Amerindian of today, he too came up from the ranks, amidst struggle and privation.

When old enough, he was enrolled in the elementary school at Fort Wingate, a land mark of Navajo history, as we have seen. There, as a bilingual child, he struggled to master simple English, unfamiliar to an Indian child's ears. But he won. A neighbor who knew Raymond's boyhood said this of him: "He was a poor boy, but he was a good boy."

Like many another of that high country, when at home he herded the family's sheep and protected them from the wolves of the wild. And there, too, he dreamed the dreams which were to make him loved among his cherished people. Later he went to Shiprock Boarding School where he completed his high school studies.

As a youth, young Raymond has been pictured to us as an inveterate reader, confirmed in his search for the best. With him the speech arts became his obsession. At the age of 24 he volunteered for service in the United States Navy — his country was at war. Aboard ship, his keen mind specialized in radiography. Thereafter over ocean's restless airwaves, he sent messages which helped to win that conflict. He saw fierce action at Guadalcanal, at Attu, at Makin, and Tarawa, facing death without fear.

Honorably discharged, Mr. Nakai married and settled in Flagstaff, Arizona, where he took up broadcasting. It proved to be a skill which stood him in good stead for tasks ahead. Soon he stood in candidacy for the leadership of his people. The chairmanship of the Great Navajo Council called loudly. He, too, stood readied. A hard fought election was on. Again, he won.

April 13, 1963 was the day of his inaugural. The platform from which he spoke carried the seventy-four members of his Navajo Nation's high council, together with the four flags and representatives of the four Rocky Mountain states into which his people's far flung reservation spread. Thousands of his fellow tribesmen stood ready to listen.

In telling language of the choicest diction, Mr. Nakai said this in conclusion: "Now as new workmen, we enter upon the great unfinished edifice of the Navajo Tribe . . . It is a better world we have to build, the one where every Navajo shall stand erect beside his fellow Americans as an equal among equals." Continuing, and with dramatic gestures, he then played his verbal trump card. He said: "Councilors and friends! The tools are ready and the task is tremendous. Let us now go to work together."[36]

Seven years have passed since that day. Raymond Nakai is still the head counselor of the Navajo Nation, the largest Indian tribe in point of numbers in the United States. Once he was a boy, dreaming on the barren wastes of the Lukuchuka country. Now his fame has spread far and wide. Today he is the head of a multi-million dollar operation, and the leader of an oncoming ambitious generation of Navajos. He is spokesman for his people's tomorrow. Who could ask for more?

America's Playlife
of the Future

ATTENTION HAS BEEN called to America's leisure bill for the year 1969. Based on present known trends, what will it be ten years hence, or even at the opening of the twenty-first century, or thereafter. So astonishing has this phase of American life become since pre-Columbian days that only the star gods, Venus, Jupiter, Mars, could venture a guess. It now stands at 83 billion dollars. By then it may pass the 100 billion dollar mark, say the fairies.

With our primeval red men, old and young, their

141

leisure time activities were many and unadorned, or we might say unsophisticated? However, they were not without zest and meaning. So, too, with the white man's frontier or pioneer life — their play media were simple but satisfying. In America's "one room" school days, youth's playground was a nearby uncultivated field, well supplied with weeds and stones.

But not so today. Even our elementary schools must have their dressed-down playgrounds, supplied with standard equipment. And as for our secondary schools, called high schools — they must have their well groomed athletic field, their tennis courts, their gymnasium, and all that goes with the specialized activities provided for the group. With the tens of thousands of such institutions, public and parochial, functioning, America's juvenile sports bills climb skyward.

And what about collegiate and professional athletics — sports of many kinds, such as baseball, football, tennis, archery, basketball, wrestling, hockey, and on and on *ad infinitum?* Also, what about the public's interest and our new national disease termed *spectatoritis* which has seized upon our American mind?

Today's Amphitheaters

What a surprise came to me personally, when I made a check on this matter! I knew that the Greeks had their open-air theatre, *Dionysius*, where they gathered to listen to their artistry and to watch their athletic sports. And as well I knew that during the proud days of the vast Roman empire its mammoth Colosseum was the gathering point for its chariot races, its gladiatorial combats, and its frolics from every part of the Mediterranean world, for I had tramped through its today's deserted quarters. But I did not know that at present there are at least one hundred

and forty American colleges and universities which have
their amphitheaters, suited to seat from 30,000 to 100,000
or more persons as watchers of their performances.

Our National Halls of Fame

And of course I knew that the United States had its
Statuary Hall, located in Washington, D.C. where each state
of the Union may place the bust of its most honored
citizen, man or woman. But until I made inquiry, I did
not know that America maintained "halls of fame" for
those who, irrespective of age, race, or color, had brought
glory to their country in bold athletic competition.

Today, those so honored, number into the thousands,
a fitting testimony of America's new day. Their postal
addresses are here given.

Aviation Hall of Fame
Dayton, Ohio
The Home of the Wright Brothers
This institution was chartered by act of Congress,
1964. Until 1969 there were but seven persons so
honored.

Baseball Hall of Fame
Cooperstown, N. Y.
It was dedicated, as an institution June 12, 1939.
Its honor roll today numbers a hundred members
or more.

Basketball Hall of Fame
Springfield, Mass.
This institution was established in 1959 as a me-
morial to James Naismith. It was in honor of the
students for Christian Workers of the previous half
century or more. Its honorees are composed of both
college and professional players of note.

College Football Hall of Fame
Rutgers University, New Brunswick, N.J.
The number of its awardees for honors is extensive, perhaps 300 or more. They represent many colleges in all parts of the United States.

Pro Football's Hall of Fame
Canton, Ohio
Its honorees come from many states of our country
as well as from many walks of life. In general its
members are adults, the game serving as their way
of making a living.

The Helms Halls of Fame
Los Angeles, Calif.
Paul H. Helms was its founder. It fixed its atten-
tion mainly on the award winners of the Olympics
of the Seven Continent members, among them are
American Indians. For the year 1912 Jim Thorpe, a
Sauk-Fox tribesman, won awards in college football,
major league football, as well as track and field sports.
In this, in truth, he was an All-American.
The following is the motto of this establishment:
"Victory is a worthy result for which to strive fairly."
It bespeaks the mind of Mr. Thorpe's forebears
continent-wide.[37]

Thus we can visualize the change which has come over
American playlife since pre-Columbian days. Then it was
simple and uninhibited, motivated primarily by two factors — worshipful attitudes toward their deities and the
development of bodily dexterity in their effort to meet
life's demands. Today it represents the growth in the number and extent of America's leisure hours, based on modern
scientific advance and technology.

Conclusion

IN OUR MENTAL TREK together in these pages, we have been made conscious of these main factors. First: We have seen the rich heritage of native American Indian recreational life, built over unnumbered centuries of time before they came into contact with the whites from across the eastern seas. Of it they have every reason to be proud. Its three categories as laid down by competent scholarship were these: amusement activities, dexterity-developing sports, and games of chance. These three types had covered the Americas before the name *Indian* was given these native sons of Columbus.

When the Spanish, the French, the English and others

came to New World shores, of course, they brought their playlife activities, as we have seen. Gradually they have fused together. Today they make up the compounded parts of our modern recreational activities. For the future our nation's problem is this: that the best in these cultures become *one*, as Raymond Nakai pled.

True — today our America is beset with many social and economic issues. However, it has ever been so with both ancient and modern life. Today we have the problem of youth's restivity, on and off of our collegiate campuses. We also have problems of urban and rural housing, difficult, indeed, to master. Likewise, matters of productive employment, of health control, of water and air pollution, of crime and legal disobedience, as well as of war service in foreign lands. All of these issues press for solution, together with many others.

However, an abiding faith resides with the American people as a whole, that together, by democratic methods, solutions to these and kindred issues will be found. But our horoscope for our cosmopolitan population tells this, if anything: patience and tested wise leadership leads the way to collective welfare at every step of human advancement, modern as well as ancient. And as the poet put it —

> Heights by great men, reached and kept,
> Were not attained by sudden flight.
> But, they, while their companions slept,
> Were toiling upward through the night.

This is our message. This is life's way. This is the abiding truth of man's upward climb toward worthy culture. Let it be America's discovery for its worthy tomorrow! "God Save America — Land We Love!"

Notes and References

1 *U.S. News & World Report.* Vol. LXVII, No. 11. September 15, 1969, pp. 58-59. Washington, D.C. Reprinted by permission.

2 The famed Cyrus E. Dillin is the sculptor here referred to. His fourth product titled "Appeal To The Great Spirit" is now the possession of The Boston Museum Of Fine Arts, Boston, Mass.

3 Louis Thomas Jones, *Aboriginal American Oratory.* Southwest Museum, Los Angeles, California, 1965, p. 125. Hereafter cited as Jones.

4 *The Royal Bank Of Canada Monthly Letter,* Vol. 47, No. 2, p. 1, Head Office, Montreal, February, 1966. With permission of The Royal Bank of Canada.

5 Twenty-Fourth Annual Report of the Bureau of American Ethnology By W. H. Holmes, 1902-1903, Washington Government Printing Office, 1907. Hereafter cited as BAER.

6 F. W. Hodge, *The Handbook Of American Indians,* Part I & II. This is a Government publication, encyclopedic in character. It was published in 1912. It can be found in most libraries of size.

147

7 BAER, 24, cited above, page 32.

8 Jones, pp. 98-99.

9 BAER, 24, pp. 36-43.

10 Lela Kiana Oman, *The Ghost of Kingikty and other Eskimo Legends,* 1967, Nome, Alaska, Ken Wray's Print Shop: Anchorage, Alaska; 1967.

11 For further information on atlatl and dart, see *Southwest Museum Leaflets* No. 4, Los Angeles, California.

12 BAER, 24, p. 485.

13 *Ibid.,* p. 87.

14 *Ibid.,* p. 229.

15 *Ibid.,* p. 231.

16 *Ibid.,* pp. 237-238.

17 *Ibid.,* p. 598.

18 *Ibid.,* pp. 599-603. Taken from George Catlin's *Letters and Notes on the Manners, Customs, and Conditions of the North American Indians* Vol. 2, p. 123, 1841.

19 *Ibid.,* p. 808. Taken from F. V. Hayden's description given in his *Ethnology and Philology of the Indian Tribes of the Mississippi Valley,* p. 430, Philadelphia, 1862.

20 Jones, p. 31.

21 Frances Densmore, *Nootka and Quileute.* Smithsonian Institution, Bureau of American Ethnology, Bulletin 24, Washington, 1939.

22 *Ibid.,* p. 236.

23 Elizabeth Waldo, *Viva California, An Early California Pastorela and Chorus,* performed by the Elizabeth Waldo Folklorica Orchestra and the St. Charles Choir, Los Angeles, California.

24 Washington Matthews, *Memoirs of the Museum of Natural History,* Vol. VI, pp. 143-145, 1902, New York, New York.

25 This address may now be obsolete. The list of songs here mentioned was acquired from a pamphlet acquired years ago. Better to contact an up-to-date music dealer for publications desired.

26 *Southwest Museum Leaflets, The Hopi Indians,* Number 25, by Ruth DeEtte Simpson, p. 77.

27 This story of Cahokia excavation is cited in the magazine *The Amerindian,* Vol. 18, No. 2, Nov.-Dec. 1969, p. 4, Chicago, Ill.

28 This account of the "57 Trail Shrines" is a remould of Paul Wilhel's thrilling article on this theme printed in *The Desert Magazine,* June, 1951, pp. 4-8, published by the Desert Press, Inc., Palm Desert, California.

29 See *Statistics Concerning Indian Education*, a pamphlet of 37 pages of educational data, published by The United States Department of Interior, Bureau of Indian Affairs, Branch of Education, p. 1, 1964.

30 Louis Thomas Jones, *Highlights Of Puebloland*, The Naylor Company, San Antonio, Tex., 1968, pp. 31-33.

31 See "Navajos Chart Educational Path," *Los Angeles Times*, p. 1, Section C, Sunday, June 1, 1969. In this article the groundwork of this Navajo institution is described.

32 See "The American Indians—Message from the President of the United States," H. Document No. 91-3630 July 8, 1970, CONGRESSIONAL RECORD H6438-6442.

33 *The Amerindian*, Vol. 18, No. 1, Sept.-Oct., 1969; Chicago, Ill., pp. 1-2, sketches Louis R. Bruce's career in brief, as he was "sworn in" as Commissioner of Indian Affairs by President Richard M. Nixon.

34 Marquis—Who's Who Inc., 200 East Ohio St., Chicago, Ill., Vol. 36; 1970-71, p. 1203.

35 *The Amerindian*, Vol. 18, No. 3, Jan.-Feb. 1970, pp. 1-2.

36 These excerpts here taken from the official copy of Raymond Nakai's Inaugural dated April 13, 1963. It represents Navajo public policy to the present.

37 This excerpt serves as the official footnote to the Helms Athletic Foundation Helms Hall stationery, August 6, 1970.

Collateral Reading

OFTEN IT IS SAID that reading is the key to learning. As we read the thoughts of others, our own views broaden. To think the thoughts of other days frequently we have to go to the printed pages. So this brief list of collateral readings is intended as an open window to the vast amount of written materials which today grace our private and public library shelves about the playlife of the American Indian of today and of pre-Columbian times. At least, it should be suggestive.

Alexander, Hartley B., *The World's Rim*, (Great Mystery of the North American Indian). University of Nebraska Press, Lincoln, 1953.

Bailey, L. P., *Indian Slave Trade In The Southwest,* Westernlore Press, Los Angeles, 1966.

Baity, Elizabeth C. *Americans Before Columbus.* The Viking Press, New York, 1961.

Daloria, Vine, Jr. *Custer Died For Your Sins.* McMillan Ltd., London, 1970.

Driver, Harold D. *The Americas On The Eve of Discovery.* Prentice-Hall, Englewood Cliff, New Jersey, 1964.

Dutton, Bertha. *Navajo Weaving Today.* Museum of New Mexico Press, Santa Fe, N. Mexico, 1961.

Eggan, Fred. *The American Indian.* Aldine Publishing Company, Chicago, 1966.

Grant, Campbell. *Rock Art of the American Indians.* Thomas Y. Crowell Co., New York, 1967.

Gridley, Marion E. *Indians of Today.* A compilation of biographies of many outstanding Indians of today's world. The 1970 Edition now available through *The Amerindian* headquarters, 1263 W. Pratt Blvd., 909, Chicago, Ill. 60626.

Jones, Louis Thomas. *So Say the Indians.* The Naylor Company, San Antonio, Texas, 1970.

Leonard, Jonathan N. *Ancient America.* Editors of Time-Life Books, New York, 1967.

Morgan, Lewis H. *Houses and House-Life of the American Aborigines.* University of Chicago Press, Chicago, 1965.

Northey, Sue. *The American Indian.* The Naylor Company, San Antonio, Texas.

Porter, C. Payne. *Our Indian Heritage.* Clinton Company, Philadelphia, Pa., 1966.

Schaafama, Polly. *Early Navaho Rock Paintings and Carvings.* Museum of Navaho Ceremonial Arts, Santa Fe, N. Mexico, 1966.

Silverberg, Robert. *Mound Builders of Ancient America.* New York Graphic Society, Greenwich, Connecticut, 1968.

Swanton, John D. *The Indian Tribes of North America.* Smithsonian Institution Press, Washington, D.C., 1968.

Wissler, Clark. *Indians of the United States.* Doubleday & Company, Garden City, New York, 1966.

Index

155

156